F.R.Foster

The Fields Were Sudden Bare

Robert Brooke

With a foreword by M.J.K.Smith

First published in Great Britain by
Association of Cricket Statisticians and Historians
Cardiff CF11 9XR
© ACS, 2011

British Library Cataloguing-in-Publication Data.
A catalogue record for this book is available from the British Library.

ISBN: 978 1 908165 02 2
Typeset by Limlow Books

Contents

Remembrances

Summer's pleasures they are gone like to visions every one,
And the cloudy days of autumn and of winter cometh on.
I tried to call them back, but unbidden they are gone
Far away from heart and eye and for ever far away.
Dear heart, and can it be that such raptures meet decay?
I thought them all eternal when by Langley Bush I lay,
I thought them joys eternal when I used to shout and play
On its bank at 'clink and bandy', 'chock' and 'taw' and 'ducking stone',
Where silence sitteth now on the wild heath as her own
Like a ruin of the past all alone.

When I used to lie and sing by old Eastwell's boiling spring,
When I used to tie the willow boughs together for a swing,
And fish with crooked pins and never catch a thing,
With heart just like a feather, now a heavy as a stone;
When beneath old Lea Close Oak I the bottom branches broke
To make our harvest cart like so many working folk,
And then to cut a straw at the brook to have a soak.
Oh, I never dreamed of parting or that trouble had a sting,
Or that pleasures like a flock of birds would ever take to wing,
Leaving nothing but a little naked spring.

Here was commons for their hills, where they seek for freedom still,
Though every common's gone and though traps are set to kill
The little homeless miners – oh, it turns my bosom chill
When I think of old Sneap Green, Puddock's Nook and Hilly Stow,
Where bramble bushes grew and the daisy gemmed in dew
And the hills of silken grass like to cushions to the view,
Where we threw the pismire crumbs when we'd nothing else to do,
All levelled like a desert by the never-weary plough,
All vanish'd like the sun where that cloud is passing now
And settled here for ever on its brow.

Oh, I never thought that joys would run away from boys,
Or that boys would change their minds and forsake such summer joys;
But alack, I never dreamed that the world had other toys
To petrify first feeling like the fable into stone,
Till I found the pleasure past and a winter come at last,
Then the fields were sudden bare and the sky got overcast,
And boyhood's pleasing haunts, like a blossom in the blast,
Was shrivelled to a withered weed and trampled down and done,
Till vanished was the morning spring and set the summer sun,
And winter fought her battle strife and won.

John Clare (1793–1864)

Foreword
by M.J.K.Smith, OBE

One major regret I have is that in my early playing days I didn't seek out and question older players about their contemporaries. In Warwickshire's case that would very much have been Sydney Barnes and Frank Foster. Present in their playing days was 'Tiger' Smith who being their keeper arguably knew more about their bowling than anyone else, and Tiger was very much a presence at Edgbaston when I started.

Foster and Barnes never played together for Warwickshire, but their performances, with Tiger keeping wicket, in Australia in 1911/12 were quite phenomenal. In the five Tests they accounted for 66 out of the 95 wickets taken – over two-thirds – and The Ashes were won. Had they both been available for the county, surely Warwickshire would have won more than their first Championship in 1911. Frank Foster never played after the war due to injury, so his career ended at 25. What a loss.

Robert sets out his record. He achieved two 'doubles' of 1,000 runs and 100 wickets in a season: he was the first man to captain the county to the Championship; and he scored the county's first triple-century, 305 not out, at quicker than a run a ball. What might he have achieved after the Great War with a full career? In cricketing terms he was still a young man, but sadly he was brought down by a serious injury in a road accident, later compounded by a major breakdown in his health.

We don't have the benefit of film footage: what a pity. Left arm fast-medium, probably a bit quicker, a good high action, pronounced nip off the wicket, the ability to swing and cut the ball, all allied to accuracy. Wickets were uncovered so that conditions would on occasions be in his favour. That he and Barnes did so well in Australia demonstrated on their good, hard tracks it was not a requirement that you had to be fast. The basics of accuracy and movement will always be the bottom line. Today's players would be intrigued by his method, round the wicket from wide of the crease with the keeper standing up – very awkward for Tiger. There was no limitation of leg-side fielders then, but since he could cut the ball back the slips would be in business. I gather he was a good slip catcher himself, so with his batting ability he was always going to be in the game. His scoring rate, making time in three-day matches made his runs even more valuable.

Have no doubt, with this ability Frank Foster would still be a major player today and a crowd-puller. We don't have him on film and have only his outstanding record as witness. In some ways, of course, I am happy that I didn't meet him when I joined Warwickshire. So I have only his cricketing achievements to associate with him rather than any reference to the distressing difficulties he experienced in his later life.

Broughton Astley, Leicestershire
January, 2011

Introduction

What would the current cricketing establishment make of Frank Rowbotham Foster? Searing fast left-arm bowler, explosive batsman with the ability to touch the stars, brilliant field, unorthodox and inspiring captain. Yet 'this gifted amateur appeared destined for greatness on the field – as long as talent could find its way to liberation through a personality which harboured more dark recesses than any ancient castle.'[1]

That Foster was a great cricketer is by no means universally accepted. Even in the bars and meeting rooms of Edgbaston, he is ranked high but not the highest. Among batsmen few allow anyone near Dennis Amiss, yet as a match winner he lags behind such figures as Brian Lara and Nick Knight. In bowling it is easier to place Eric Hollies top, though some suggest Allan Donald as a serious rival. All these players were backed by figures. For wicket-keepers it is difficult to judge; his contemporaries reckoned Dick Lilley was unexcelled, yet few who saw him can imagine a finer keeper than Keith Piper.

But with regard to allrounders, Frank Foster is Warwickshire's best, with no real challengers. In 127 county matches Foster scored 5,436 runs, av. 27.04 and took 587 wickets, av. 20.57. Only five other allrounders with any sort of career did so well all round that their batting average exceeded their bowling. They were W.G.Quaife, 33,862 runs (36.17), 900 wickets (27.53) in 665 matches; R.E.S.Wyatt 21,687 runs (41.54), 652 wickets (32.82) in 404 matches; T.W.Cartwright 10,780 runs (22.09), 1,058 wickets (18.75) in 353 matches; D.R.Brown 8,066 runs (30.90), 515 wickets (29.79) in 197 matches; and A.F.Giles 3,297 runs (30.24), 323 wickets (26.19) in 100 matches. Actually these figures are misleading; only Foster was a genuine allrounder match after match, throughout a career. Yet can one quantify allround skills and effectiveness on bald figures? Some have tried.

In *The Cricket Society News Bulletin* for November 2007, Keith Walmsley attempted to establish a system for calculating the best allround figures during an English season. Walmsley awarded one point for each run scored, ten for every wicket taken and added them together. Most points indicated the best allround season but the method was unsatisfactory since the more matches played meant more points were likely to accrue. Then there were players who scored a huge number of runs and took a few wickets like Denis Compton and Bill Edrich in 1947. Their inflated totals certainly were not owed to allround worth. However, that George Hirst, by a long way, has the highest ever points total for a county season, when he

---

1   Brian Halford, *Birmingham Mail*, in unpublished MS on the 1911 season.

exceeded 2,000 runs and 200 wickets in 1906, proves the Walmsley method has some merit, but I felt dividing the points total by number of matches to reach an average, the higher the average the better the season, brought about a more acceptable, albeit still unfair result. Compton and Edrich remain inordinately high, but were now separated by W.G.Grace and J.W.Hearne, while in fifth position is Frank Foster, who in 1911 actually exceeded George Hirst *pro rata*. Taking into account that Foster bowled fast, whereas Hearne was gentle slow, and Foster led Warwicks to its first title, I submit the case for suggesting Frank Foster in 1911 enjoyed the most effective allround season in the history of the County Championship. Of course nothing can be proven. I still think that, for a 22-year-old non-Test cricketer, his 1911 performances almost defy belief.

Leading Allrounders in a Season (Walmsley Method)

Player/ county	Year	Mt	Runs	Wx10	Pts	Ave
D.C.S.Compton (Midd)	1947	19	2467	630	3097	163.00
W.G.Grace (Glos)	1887	14	1405	640	2045	146.07
J.W.Hearne (Middx)	1914	22	2021	1140	3161	143.68
W.J.Edrich (Middx)	1947	22	2650	500	3150	143.18
F.R.Foster (Warks)	1911	20	1459	1240	2699	134.95
F.E.Woolley (Kent)	1921	22	1637	1290	2927	133.05
G.H.Hirst (Yorks)	1906	32	2164	2010	4174	130.44
J.W.Hearne (Middx)	1920	22	1637	1230	2867	130.32
C.L.Townsend (Glos)	1899	21	1908	770	2678	127.52

Warwickshire Allrounders in a Season (Walmsley Method)

Player	Year	Mt	Runs	Wx10	Pts	Ave
F.R.Foster	1911	20	1459	1240	2699	134.95
F.R. Foster	1914	24	1396	1170	2566	106.92
R.E.S.Wyatt	1929	25	1953	530	2483	99.32
R.E.S.Wyatt	1928	27	2075	500	2575	95.37
Hon F.S.G.Calthorpe	1921	22	1239	820	2059	93.59

An older method of ranking allrounders was the brainchild of George Wood, a professional statistician, who published his results in various issues of *The Cricketer* of 1938 and 1939. Wood's figures were updated by Martyn Taylor in issues of *The Cricket Statistician* in 1974 and 1975, while I covered the period from Taylor's update to the present day.

Wood's methods were complicated, and involved mathematical calculation and comparison throughout a whole career to finally reach a 'value' but, for those who can stomach everything being reduced to 'pure' statistics, the leaders in the Wood rankings were F.A.Tarrant with 7.97, R.J.Hadlee with 7.95, W.G.Grace on 7.33 S.G.Smith on 6.85 and, in fifth position, Foster himself with 5.95. Behind him in the rankings were G.H.Hirst on 5.89, G.S.Sobers on 5.51, M.J.Procter 5.48, G.A.Lohmann 5.21, G.J.Thompson 5.20. F.E.Woolley 5.14, J.N.Crawford 5.14 and Wilfred Rhodes on 5.03.

(I.T.Botham achieved 3.95 on the scale.) Again, the higher the value, the more effective the allrounder. I do not pretend this table proves anything, but it has to be said that Frank Foster comes out of things quite well. The leading Warwickshire players, both well behind Foster, were A.F.Giles with 3.73 and T.W.Cartwright with 2.95.

Finally, with regard to Foster's position for Warwicks, it may be of interest that in 2007 an 'All-Time Eleven' was selected to celebrate 125 years of the club, chosen by members, from a list drawn up by a panel. Foster, Tom Cartwright and Dermot Reeve were classified as 'allrounders' and the panel, in its wisdom, decreed only one allrounder be selected. The members understandably chose the player they remembered best, so two of Warwicks' greatest were omitted. The whole thing was an embarrassing farce. Despite 'expert' views I claim that Frank Foster was the greatest Warwicks cricketer ever.

Chapter One
Warwick, thou art worthy

Punch magazine dated 6 September 1911 printed a cartoon by F.H.Townsend showing Foster being congratulated by William Shakespeare, a Warwickshire qualified playwright, and whose speed in pursuit of Thomas Lucy's deer suggested a natural outfielder. Foster addresses the Bard, 'Tell Kent from me she hath lost.' (Kent were the only challengers at the end.) Shakespeare replies, 'Warwick, thou art worthy.' The quotations are taken, out of context of course, from Parts II and III of Henry VI and are delightfully apt.

Though he could pen a lively sentence or two, and was also Warwicks qualified, Frank Foster was not a *littérateur* of Shakespearian standard. Indeed in the 1930s he could not find a publisher for his second set of memoirs. Some of this material is still extant[2] and record his thoughts on Warwicks winning the County Championship in 1911 and various related matters.

This is what he wrote:

'Frank, art thou sitting around all morning?'
'Tha' sounds real Yorkshire, and yes I am.'

Thus, Mel Valley, Moseley,[3] 25 August 1911, 11.00 am and the start of the most memorable hundred hours of my life. I am in my dressing room, still in dressing-gown and starting a second pipeful. Later I will be catching the LNWR to Northampton to lead my Warwickshire team to its first-ever cricket title. Presently though, there is no hurry; I can relax and here is father mythering on. He'll have me exercising the horses next. Little wonder I annoy him by mentioning his now almost undetectable Yorkshire accent.[4]

He is really a lovely gentleman to whom I owe everything. He has a great sense of humour and is remarkably patient and tolerant – as he needs to be having four wild sons with whom to contend. I shortly wash and dress, and join father, mother and sister Florence for luncheon. I can eat little and it is with relief that I pile my luggage onto father's carriage

---

2   At one time, the library at the Edgbaston ground held a copy.
3   Mel Valley was the name of the Foster family home, incorporating a Hackney pony stud run by our subject's father. See Chapter Two.
4   It is slightly surprising that Frank Foster referred to Yorkshire since although William Foster had lived and been in business in the Pontefract area, he was from a Lincolnshire family. Maybe a slight 'Northern' accent may have been an appropriate description.

and he drives me to New Street Station. I first pay my respects to The Dell replete as ever with dragonflies and honeysuckles in its haunted glades. I better keep friendly with the spirits that dwell there.[5] Seeing me off onto the train are Colonel Wilkinson and Mr C.S.Riddell,[6] my bosses, and Mr Ryder and Mr Bainbridge from Warwickshire.[7] Most important of course, my lovely players are there.

Word has come through that rain has prevented play at Canterbury; if it stays like that Kent are out of contention. Unfortunately at Lord's Middlesex are steamrollering Hampshire. 'Don't worry skipper,' says good old Frank Field, 'we'll beat Northampton and it doesn't matter.' 'And God bless Mr Sewell,' I say, referring to a London journalist who disapproves of us.[8]

Father hugs me: 'Play hard but fair Frank; you can do it; remember you are a Foster.' A supporter asked me if we were going to win. 'We'll paralyse them' I replied. A toot and a cloud of steam from our locomotive, a little cheer from the assembled supporters, and off we go. A pity Sep Kinneir is lame and sad and stayed behind. 'Win it for him,' I tell my lads. After all Sep had scored lots of runs and supported my craziest notions.

Northampton is a small market town, the ground a little way out. We rose early Saturday morning[9] and walked to the ground. I was feeling edgy but seeing the sun shining cheered me up. Probably in the whole history of county cricket there had never been played a match of such great importance. Warwickshire, since the commencement of their cricketing life, had never reached a position so high as the one they held prior to this match and the tremendous effect of winning this match on the Birmingham public was so intense that I was absolutely determined to make the greatest effort ever known in the history of cricket. I knew my men were with me, heart and soul, and that no words of mine could make them try harder than the effort they were now prepared to make for the honour of winning the County Championship for Warwickshire.

Ten good men and true are with me inspecting the wicket. The day is hot, the wicket perfect, thunder in the air. Best to bat and get it over with quick as we can, I thought. 'Toss 'em for the match, skipper, you'll win.' says Jack Parsons, full of youthful optimism. I smiled and went to

---

5   'The Dell' would have been the site of 'Moseley Bog'. See Chapter Two.
6   Partners in the furnishing firm Wilkinson and Riddell, based in Cherry Street, Birmingham, where Foster worked when not playing cricket. The business remained in existence in Birmingham until the 1950s.
7   Warwickshire County Cricket Club secretary and chairman respectively.
8   E.H.D.Sewell was an amateur batsman for Essex and other mainly southern sides and a cricket author whose trenchant views, often assertions rather than reasoned arguments, demeaned him as a writer.
9   Saturday starts had not yet been generally adopted, but this one favoured Warwicks.

meet the opposing captain, G.A.T. ('Tubby') Vials. 'Nice day.' I said. 'Stormy weather about,' he replied. 'It looks like it. Shall we toss?'

The walk to the middle seemed so long, but not so long as the walk back. We tossed, and I lost. My heart sank into my boots. A perfect wicket, a Saturday start, rain threatening, and certain by Monday, Northamptonshire a good batting side but with Syd Smith[10] a great wet-wicket bowler. Can you wonder at my dream of failure? We *have* to win, but how?

I went round to speak to my boys. 'You won the toss, skipper?' they shouted. I shook my head. A deathly silence prevailed in the dressing-room for what seemed fully two minutes. 'Lost it?' enquired Frank Field, whose lion-hearted fast bowling had done so much to put us on top. 'What good are you?' he went on. 'Never mind skipper, you leave 'em to me. I'll bowl 'em out. YOU can't bowl, you never could'.

I walked away thinking the end of the world. To get so near, and yet so far. Is it fate or is it Providence? God must decide the issue, but then I do believe in God.

Warwickshire took the field and commenced the first day's play. Before lunch Northants were all out! Things could hardly have gone better. I started things off when William Denton missed my third ball of the match – a straight 'un – and lost his middle stump, or his off stump. (Who cares? He was out.) Frank Field was our hero however, slicing through the Northants batting like a hot knife through butter. In no time at all they were 67 for six, four in succession to Frank, and our joy was unalloyed when Syd Smith ran out George Thompson since they were their best batters. Syd was still fuming with himself when Frank Field had him nicking to 'my' Tiger.[11] I had decided to rest myself, telling Willie Hands[12] to 'do some work for a change', but now sensed good figures. The last four batters surrendered to me and the home team were all out 73 in only 34.2 overs. The lads strolled off to lunch light of heart, and I telegraphed father with the news.

We too started badly. George Thompson,[13] still smarting over his run out, quickly bowled 'Tiger' but then Frank Stephens and Crow Charlesworth added 82 and at the close we were 153 runs in front, and still four wickets left. Charlesworth, playing the innings of his life, was unbeaten with 113 but most of us did our bit – except me. Syd Smith could not forgive my running out Thompson. He bowled a terrible ball, I

---

10   S.G.Smith, a left-handed all-rounder and an early West Indian import.
11   E.J. 'Tiger' Smith who, in a playing career extending to 1930, appeared in over 400 matches for Warwicks and eleven for England. Later a first-class umpire, standing in over 200 matches, including eight Tests, he became the county's coach and was still attending matches at Edgbaston in 1979.
12   William Cecil Hands was known as 'Cecil' according to his family, but Foster always called him 'Willie'.
13   George Thompson, fine allrounder, and Northamptonshire's first Test cricketer.

yelled 'that's easy Syd' and hit it high to Fanny Walden on the leg boundary. That made me feel thoroughly fed up. (I made a duck.)

At the close I sent father another telegraph: 'We are on our way there.' We felt light of heart that night, but next day, Sunday, it rained incessantly. The bad weather made us nervous. Middlesex had well overcome Hampshire at Lord's (no surprise there) but how could Yorkshire have allowed Kent to beat them in a game of less than two full days play? 'Shouldn't rely on Yorkshire, they're no good,' averred our Red Rose pair Charlie Baker and Crow Charlesworth. 'I was nearly a Yorkshireman,' I reminded them.[14] 'Anyway skipper, we are going to win, so who cares?' Frank Field talking of course, 'Though we could have done with some runs from our No.5. Who was he?' I chased him and threw my pipe at him. We played poker, bridge, any old game. We laughed, talked, told every tale which came out of the ark. We enjoyed simply being alive – laughing in the face of fate.

On Monday the ground was too wet for the resumption. Lunch came and by then we were all of a very sober turn of mind. We commenced about 3 o'clock. Charlesworth soon fell for 130 – he was in for 210 minutes and hit 17 fours; what a great innings. Syd Smith got him, and the other three wickets. He loved the rain-affected pitch, but so too, we hoped would our bowlers. Warwickshire's innings closed at 281. When Northamptonshire went in I was again lucky enough to get William Denton in the first over. His partner was skipper Tubby Vials, promoting himself from No.5. 'That's all right skipper, he can't see,' reckoned Frank Field, 'I'll give him a straight 'un.' Sure enough he did get Vials with a 'straight 'un' that uprooted his middle peg but only after Vials had stayed for two hours, and 30 runs. Vials added 52 with Seymour and was there over after over (not bad for someone who couldn't see) and as the close loomed, and with the uncertain weather, we were becoming all 'hot and bothered'. We were encouraged when Field dismissed Vials but when play finished for the day there were still three Northamptonshire wickets to fall.

Our one and only danger was further rain. We actually spent the night in ordinary clothes, playing cards, singing songs, everything. It was the longest night of my life, but I could never have slept. Then daylight dawned, and we saw the perfect cricket morning; a beautiful clear sky, not a sign of rain. I took the bowling with Frank Field and immediately bowled Walden (140 for eight). John Denton was then joined by James Ryan, a new boy looking fresh out of school. He and Denton became an annoyance; they added 34 before I got one on Denton's pads, with the batsman getting into a real tangle. 'Out,' said the umpire; Denton was terribly disappointed, but had no need to feel guilty, he had played

---

14   This is probably true since his elder brother Harry was Yorkshire-born. One wonders how cricket history may have been changed had the Fosters stayed in Pontefract another two or three years. For one thing Yorkshire may well have had an amateur skipper who was worth his place.

really well. Buswell now joined Ryan, and only a further single was added before I put everything into a delivery, and what a beauty it was, moving away in the air then straightening. Ryan groped, the off stump was out of the ground, the young lad was bowled, Northamptonshire all out. 'We are champions!' I yelled.

Among the first to congratulate me was my last victim. 'Top hole, Mr. Foster, that ball was too good for me,' he said, as he shook my hand. Ryan had played bravely and well. Sadly this was the pinnacle of his career, his cricket career that is. Four years later Captain Ryan, Military Cross and Mentioned in Despatches, still only 22, fell leading his men at Loos in France. His sportsmanship and friendliness in our victory, and the manner of his death while so young confirmed 'This was a Man.'

As we walked off, a crowd of about 200, mostly it seemed Warwickshire supporters, surged onto the pitch to greet us. Prominent amongst them was father, who came and hugged me. He was speechless and I am sure I saw tears in his eyes. I mentioned this to him later: 'Rubbish, Yorkshiremen don't show their feelings like that.'

When we reached the pavilion we were met by the Northamptonshire secretary Mr A.J.Darnell, replete in silk 'topper' who delivered an impromptu speech congratulating us. He remarked that our players had comported themselves so well, and with such dignity he hoped we would be the opposition when Northamptonshire took their first title. Poor Mr Darnell; years later he was still wearing the 'topper', still awaiting that title.

We had a champagne supper in the pavilion. Someone suggested 'Mr Foster must make a speech.' Mr Foster did, but father William, not Frank who by this time was 'sleeping it off' in a corner, wrapped around his best mate Frank Field.

We were taken back to our hotel in a 'four-in-hand' complete with post-horn, of which I took charge, though everyone else 'wanted a blow'. From there a now slightly bedraggled, dishevelled group was taken to the Castle railway station, and so back to Birmingham. There was more 'merry-making' on the 2.29 from Northampton and when we arrived in Birmingham there was no 'sham' about the 'pain' in our heads, nor was there anything sham about the enthusiasm shown the team by the Birmingham public. Several thousand greeted us in Queen's Drive,[15] from where a fleet of motor cars took us to the Grand Hotel.[16] There, more alcoholic sustenance and speeches. My joy was unbounded. I will always remember Northampton as giving me the greatest day of my life.[17]

---

15   A public thoroughfare in those days dividing New Street Station.
16   A fine Victorian building sadly almost derelict in 2010.
17   An unnerving statement given the place Northampton was to play in his later life.

Foster's men.
The Warwickshire side which beat Northamptonshire by an innings at Northampton on 26, 28 and 29 August 1911, thus winning the Championship. Standing (l to r): C.Charlesworth, C.S.Baker, E.B.Crockford (twelfth man), E.F.Field, J.H.Parsons, S.Santall, E.J.Smith (wk). Seated: W.G.Quaife, G.W.Stephens, F.R.Foster (capt), F.G.Stephens, W.C.Hands.

Even if we make allowance for possible intervention by a ghost writer, it is a remarkable passage. Writing in the 1930s he is trying to recollect, in a singularly unbuttoned way, the intensity of his feelings – 'joys eternal when I used to shout and play' – when he skippered Warwicks to the Championship in the bright, Edwardian summer of 1911 (despite the weather in this particular match) more than twenty years before. At that time the Championship was a major prize in the English sporting calendar. In winning it, Warwicks had toppled the cosy cartel of the 'big six' counties who had won the competition every season since W.G.Grace's outsiders, Gloucestershire, had led the field. What's more it was his first season as appointed captain, though that achievement is not so rare. He was, at 22, the youngest captain to take the title – he remains so. He had done the double – 1,000 runs and 100 wickets – in championship matches alone; no other winning captain has done that. To judge from the tone of these particular 'Remembrances', he had achieved it more by collaborative means than by the traditional 'officers and subordinates' method of management.

But he was viewing it across the wreckage of his own life. He had been injured in a road accident in 1915 and had contributed little to the convulsive efforts of the Great War. He had been pushed out of the family's business, was separated from his wife and children, had been involved in some 'funny stuff' in Soho, had a serious gambling habit and was heading for bankruptcy.

Now read on, please do.

TWO GENTLEMEN OF WARWICKSHIRE.

A cartoon published in Punch magazine of
6 September 1911 celebrating Warwickshire's
championship title.
The rest of the caption read: Mr F.R.Foster (Captain of
the Warwickshire XI, who have just won the Cricket
Championship): 'Tell Kent from me she hath lost.'
William Shakespeare: 'Warwick, thou art worthy.'

Chapter Two

The first 'Foster Brother'

William Foster, born at Billingham in Lincolnshire of farming stock in 1853, was the sort of self-made entrepreneur who would have delighted Mrs Thatcher a hundred and more years later. While still young he moved to Pontefract and dabbled in various business enterprises. His successes as a dealer in bankrupt stock, auctioneer and estate agent were somewhat mixed – indeed he once ran up considerable debts which he subsequently repaid – but there can be no disputing his expertise as a gentleman's outfitter. He opened his first 'Foster Brothers' shop[18] at Beastfair in the West Riding town of Pontefract in 1876. In 1879 he married Elizabeth Rowbotham, one of the six daughters of Henry Rowbotham, a Pontefract schoolmaster (though originally from Macclesfield) and his wife Elizabeth, who was herself born in Chipping, on the edge of the Forest of Bowland, in Lancashire. The union produced four sons and two daughters. They lived at Friarwood Road, Pontefract and by 1881 had a servant. However it seems William wished to expand his business horizons and in 1884 he opened a shop at 414 Coventry Road, Small Heath, a couple of miles east of Birmingham city centre.[19] The family lived over the shop and that is where, in the county of Warwickshire (giving him a birth qualification to play cricket for the county) on 31 January 1889, second son Frank Rowbotham was born.[20]

Foster Brothers continued to expand apace after William's death in 1914. Though remaining a Midland company (a new head office was opened in Solihull in 1968) and family orientated – oldest son Harry and third son Edgar were working directors for many years and Frank's son John eventually became joint managing director – more than 700 branches opened nationally. Swallowed up in 1985 by a conglomerate, Sears PLC, the Foster Brothers name disappeared for ever, but is still remembered by men dragged there in their youth by their parents when they would possibly have preferred something a little trendier.

---

18   Despite the 'Brothers' appellation there were, strictly speaking, no brothers but William thought it sounded better. The business, which predated Burton's, was among the earliest of multiple retailers of menswear.

19   It is unclear why Birmingham was chosen; there was no apparent connection with the West Midlands though William's parents moved to Nuneaton, where they lived into their nineties.

20   Other sources claim Deritend as Frank Foster's birthplace, but although this was the registration sub-district there is no doubt whatsoever that it was Small Heath. In 2011 a branch of the British Islamic Bank occupies the site, a modern building perhaps less than thirty years old. Adding to the confusion, the 1891 Census gives his birthplace as Bordesley, nearer to the Birmingham city centre, and with its own railway station, but this could not possibly be correct.

Foster Brothers' first shop in Beastfair, Pontefract, photographed in the 1940s.

A very comfortable life.
Mel Valley, Foster's childhood home, off Wake Green Road, Moseley, in its heyday.

After living in Birmingham for a few years William Foster decided to develop his other major interest – the breeding of Hackney ponies. For use as a stud, he bought Mel Valley,[21] a substantial, two-storeyed house standing in its own grounds, on the Wake Green Road at Moseley. The property, about four miles south-east of Birmingham city centre, appears on an 1883 plan of the area as a large building set back from the road, while there is also a lodge, and much land. He could hardly have chosen anywhere more likely to feed the imagination of his fantasy-prone second son Frank. It was close to the atmospheric Sarehole Mill, so beloved of J.R.R.Tolkien, and overlooked what became Moseley Bog, the site of a reservoir associated with the mill but these days a local nature reserve, partly wooded, with an atmosphere all its own. This writer explored it alone in 2010; and although it is now of limited size, not much more than twenty acres say, it seemed to expand almost to infinity. Archaeological exploration on the site reveals human activity back to the Bronze Age. Tolkien was living only 100 yards or so from Mel Valley when William Foster took it over and knew Moseley Bog as 'the Dell', as indeed did Frank Foster. Tolkien would certainly have known Mel Valley after being brought from South Africa and it is surely likely that he drew inspiration from here for the ponies featuring in *Lord of the Rings*. William Foster became a respected judge of horse flesh, in countries as far flung as the United States and Argentina, and shortly before his death in 1914, aged 61, had supplied a team of ponies to the Vanderbilts in Pennsylvania. Right up to 1915 the Mel Valley string was shown at venues such as Madison Square Garden.

William Foster was involved in football, and had been a committeeman with Birmingham F.C. at his death, but his main sporting interest was cricket. Although no record exists of his playing the game, he became a Warwickshire committee member and his sons all played. William became President of Hall Green C.C. and at the end of several seasons raised his own 'Mel Valley' team to play them. Oldest son Harry did well for Hall Green, in 1906 taking 60 wickets at less than four apiece. Arthur, for some mysterious reason played once for Warwickshire in 1914, while Edgar played at The Leys School in Cambridge. None however could ever approach second brother Frank, a cricketing genius who had it within him to be one of the greatest ever allrounders. How easy, and boring, would it have been had things run smoothly.

---

21   In the 1920s and 1930s, Mel Valley, still occupied by Elizabeth Foster and several servants, was numbered 204 Wake Green Road: the Lodge was 214. After the Second World War, No. 204 became an educational establishment and also an old peoples' home. There is now no trace of either 204 or 214 but, working from old maps, it would seem that Mel Valley stood a few yards the Sarehole side of the modern St Bernard's Catholic Primary School. The forbidding presence of Moseley Bog looms and I feel it likely that part of the Mel Valley land now belongs to Moseley Bog and indeed there remain traces of possible stabling on the Bog. Mel Valley first appears in a Birmingham Directory for 1890. Before William Foster moved in about 1898 it was occupied by Mr B.C.Tipper, animal food manufacturer; his son Benjamin Clarke Cecil Tipper played for Worcestershire in 1919. This unexpected cricket connection seems slightly weird.

Chapter Three
Early Years

Frank Foster was a true 'Brummie' and a poor recording of a speech about 'Bodyline' suggests a trace of the Brummie 'whine', noticeable in another distinguished native born a couple of miles away as the crow flies, Enoch Powell, and now largely kept alive, at least in intelligible form, among Birmingham people of Asian origin.

As William Foster became more successful he took his family to Mel Valley, where he could indulge his pastime of breeding Hackney ponies, and give his children large grounds in which to play. The first we hear of the family's cricket interest is in some notes by Frank Foster for an unpublished autobiography. Foster had played truant from school and so omitted to give his teacher a letter from his mother saying they were to take a two-week holiday. On his return home 'at the normal time' so as to keep his truancy secret, 'on the lawn my father, brother and sister are playing cricket. Dad calls out for me to field for him by the hedge. I hide the letter in a thick part of the hedge and within five minutes the ball is sent straight to me. Could I stop it? Oh dear no, and the ball nestled close to my guilt. Could I get it out? I could not. Someone else found it and the letter, and Frankie is sent to bed to await developments.'

William Foster used to tell a story of the young Frank's keenness. When Frank was about six, his mother, looking out one day from an upstairs window, saw the boy throwing a ball against a wall, and catching it as it fell. She watched for some time, unseen by him, and noticed that Frank's eyes were full of tears, and he was muttering 'I will do it! I will do it!' Later she discovered he was determined to take a hundred catches without a miss – remarkable for one of his age. William realised that Frank possessed cricketing ability denied the other Fosters and throughout the long summer evenings would organise cricket practice. Frank would spend much time bowling at a single stump. Father would place a penny on the stump, another on a length and if Frank dislodged both coins he won them, plus another sixpence from the proud, albeit poorer father. This practice, and parental encouragement, fused to huge natural talent, gave Frank Foster the self-confidence and aplomb to step into any grade of cricket without difficulty.

When Frank was a small boy the family holidayed at Saltburn-by-the-Sea, Yorkshire, where there was an immense stretch of sand ideal for playing cricket. One morning Frank won half a crown from his father bowling at a single stump and, according to Frank, was seen by members of the Saltburn Cricket Club who chose him, aged about seven, in their team to play

Foster's parents, William and Elizabeth, two strong personalities. William was managing director of the Foster Brothers' menswear business until his death in 1914; Elizabeth chaired the company from 1918 to 1943.

Saltburn visitors, who included Basil Foster of the Worcestershire brotherhood. 'Basil made a stupendous score but what I couldn't understand was every time he hit a six or boundary he sat down and rested under the umpire's coat. I could not understand what his game was until someone told me he suffered with his heart. That, I think, explains why Basil never attained the success gained by his brothers.' This particular Foster reappears later in Frank's story.

Aged ten, Frank became a boarder at Solihull Grammar School,[22] where he showed such cricketing ability that in 1902 he was appointed captain of the school team, and remained so until he left, aged fifteen, in 1904. He once remarked that he owed all his cricket to Solihull, and it would certainly have helped that whilst there he was coached by Frank Shacklock and Light, the school professionals and by the ex-Warwicks player Charles Cort.[23] He was also a member of the school Cadet Corps. Whether he appreciated the discipline instilled here is not known, but he certainly disliked the Latin and Greek which all pupils had to study.

---

22   Founded in 1560, it became an independent day school, as Solihull School, in 1946 and in 1948 joined the Headmasters' Conference. Remarkable for its diversity, former pupils include poets Richard Jago and William Shenstone; diplomat Sir Oliver Wright; banker Sir Derek Higgs; former FA chairman Sir Bert Millichip; ex-Tory M.P. Andrew Mackay; late Communist Party of Great Britain organiser Dave Cook; Olympic skater John Curry; champion boxer Wally Swift, jun; 1992 television 'Mastermind' Steve Williams; classical musicians James Barralet and Laurence Cummings; and, sticking to the music theme, Genesis P. Orridge of Throbbing Gristle. Latest addition to the Warwicks cricketers' list begun with Frank Foster is Richard Johnson.

23   Frank Shacklock was a fast bowler with Nottinghamshire and Derbyshire before emigrating to New Zealand. Light is likely to have been Elisha Light, a Hampshire professional until 1900; he later played for Carmarthenshire. Charles Cort was a pace bowler who appeared for Warwicks in 1887 and 1888.

In his mid-teens Frank joined elder brother Harry with Hall Green Cricket Club, not far from the family's home, and in 1906 he took 70 wickets and averaged 22 to win the batting prize. Next season he scored his maiden century and also played twice for Poulton while holidaying on the Lancashire coast. Against Blackpool he scored 64 and took six for 14; against a Garstang side including Lancashire players Joe and Alex Eccles he made ten and took four for 10. Back in Birmingham, he played for 'The Arcadians', a team got up by Wilkinson and Riddell, Frank's employers, who traded in Great Western Arcade, Birmingham. His figures of nine for nine against 'The Rest of the Warehouse' won Frank a bat from C.S.Riddell, one of the partners. His abilities were becoming known, and at Whitsun 1908, Joe Phillips[24] was told to include him in Warwicks' Second Eleven game with Worcestershire. Secretary R.V.Ryder informed Phillips: 'This boy slings them down left-handed.'[25] Give him a trial and see what you think of him. He's no bat.' Foster took five for 25 and two for 19, and, going in last, scored a quickfire unbeaten 51, adding more than 100 for the last wicket with A.J.Woodward.[26]

---

24   Joe Phillips, a colliery manager and occasional amateur player and skipper for Warwicks, became, years after his death the first grandfather-in-law of H.R.H. Princess Anne, and great-grandfather of champion horsewoman Zara Phillips.

25   Fred Root, a fellow leg-theorist, writing in 1937, described his bowling action as 'loose-limbed' and 'care-free'. He thought him a 'holy terror' because he frequently hit batsmen on 'the tender part of the thigh'.

26   The unfortunate Woodward was chosen for Warwicks' first-team home fixture with Leicestershire later in the season. It was rained off and he never played first-class cricket.

Chapter Four
Young cricketer making his way

Cricket magazine – it styled itself a 'weekly record of the game' – reported on 2 July 1908 that 'F.R.Foster, a useful batsman and slow left-hand bowler from Hall Green made his debut for Warwicks in this match and obtained six wickets.' Not quite accurate but Foster's first appearance was duly noted. The opponents were Derbyshire at the Racecourse Ground in Derby on 25, 26 and 27 June and he replaced Fred Moorhouse from the team beaten by Yorkshire the day before. Skipper was Tom Fishwick, a frequent deputy but never officially appointed joint-captain, despite what some Warwicks records claim. When the 'proper' skipper deigned to play, Fishwick reverted to being an ordinary team member, yet his captaincy record was better than any he understudied.

Foster was fortunate that Wilkinson and Riddell allowed him time off to play. In unpublished autobiographical notes Foster describes a meeting with C.S.Riddell, one of the partners:

> I remember Mr C.S.Riddell saying some nice words to me and wishing me the best of luck for my 'Derby Day'. He also gave me six stamped telegraph forms to send off to him at each lunch and tea interval. I think I am correct in saying that owing to nervousness I hadn't the pluck to go near the telegraph office so I destroyed those six wires. I was only a baby and very sensitive.

Foster also described how one of his jobs was sweeping the floor each night. Once in some horseplay he threw a bundle of stockings at a work mate, only to land a bulls-eye on Colonel Howard Wilkinson, the other partner. '"Are you the cricketer?" the Colonel said. "No sir." I replied. "Dear me, how very unfortunate," laughed the Colonel as he walked away.

*New boy.
Foster, aged 19, in his first season with Warwickshire*

Fishwick won the toss and batted. Warwicks' first three were Quaife, Kinneir and Baker – 'slow and sure' Foster described them – who were unlikely to empty the bars but they ensured a good score, 428 in 146 overs. With Derbyshire collapsing and following on, Warwicks were victorious by ten wickets. The tyro played his part. He scored only seven but made a dream start with the ball. Derbyshire were 24 for three, Foster taking two of them.

His victims were skipper L.G.Wright, a fine player albeit a veteran, and nuggety pro Sam Cadman. Neither was likely to sell his wicket cheaply and at lunch Wright said to Foster: 'I predict that if you are half as good as Sydney Barnes you will play for England. Barnes was the first man to obtain my wicket in County cricket and now you come along and obtain it in your first match. Furthermore with your next ball you obtain the wicket of Sam Cadman.'[27]

Derbyshire reached 185, Billy Quaife taking the last five wickets with his slow, flighted non-turners. Foster took no more wickets, Fishwick wisely not submitting him to too much exposure, but two for 14, in 15 overs, looked impressive. Derbyshire, mainly due to a century from L.G.Wright, fought hard after following on but at 216 for four, Foster, whose opening spell had been unproductive, returned. 216 for four became 256 all out, and Foster's final and decisive spell saw him take four of the last five wickets for nine runs. Six wickets, a match-winning spell – the real outcome was the discovery of a new star in the firmament.

He retained his place for the next four matches. Against Surrey at The Oval, Hayward and Hobbs were in cracking form and the former hit a fine century as they belaboured the bowling, Foster included, but he did get both their wickets as his county forced an unlikely draw. Foster's home debut was against Hampshire; some aggressive pace bowling by Frank Field which brought him five wickets put the home side in the driving seat, but Foster gave good support with three for 35. Foster managed only one second-innings wicket and was dismissed for two by Buck Llewellyn, the coloured South African Test player, but Warwicks needed only 52 for victory.

It was then up to Blackpool to take on Lancashire, and a first experience of the dismal side of county cricket. Rain, gloom, a poor wicket, yet memorable for Foster who first knock dismissed Archie Spooner, Jack Sharp, A.H.Hornby, Huddleston and Harry Dean for his first five-wicket haul. Unfortunately workaday medium-pacer Willie Huddleston found conditions perfect; thirteen wickets for 112 was a career best and won the game for his side. Foster's final outing was against Northamptonshire at Edgbaston, playing a quiet but important role with second innings figures of three for 29 in an innings victory.[28]

Foster was also selected for the Leicestershire game at Coventry but rain allowed not a single ball to be bowled. Disappointing for him, since he

---

27 Actually this was complete fiction. Wright played his first county match in 1883 and was dismissed in both innings by the one-eyed, tragically short-lived Sussex left-armer 'Jumper' Juniper. Presumably he was simply encouraging our subject. Wright remembered his debut well enough in his memoirs, reporting that Juniper was 'a big man with a shade over one eye'.

28 Apropos nothing, the Northamptonshire openers were Freeman and Hardy, while in 1919 Willis made an appearance. Apart from this being appropriate to the shoe county, those to whom such things appeal may like to know that Freeman Hardy and Willis shoe shops were eventually swallowed up by Sears PLC, as were Foster Brothers.

knew he would now have to return to the day job, but more so for local amateur A.J.Woodward who, as reported earlier, never did play first-class cricket.

So Frank went back to to the hosiery trade and to Hall Green CC with a first-class record of 170.5 overs, 44 maidens, 397 runs and 23 wickets at an average 17.26: a few months later *Wisden* listed him as the top Warwicks bowler and sixteenth in its national averages. He gave little evidence of latent batting talent, but it had been an impressive start.

1909 unfolded with a visit to Surrey at The Oval, and no other suitable amateur being available, the captaincy devolved upon Russell Everitt[29] of Moseley, and a thin looking attack was bolstered by the now 20-year-old Frank Foster. Surrey, for whom Hayward and Hobbs produced a first wicket stand of 352, still their best against Warwicks, quite outplayed the visitors to win easily. Foster had 'none for plenty' and perhaps learned there was more to county cricket than he had realised, but he did attain his maiden first-class fifty, in about an hour, ensuring the follow-on was narrowly avoided. A visit to Derby was notable only for the fact that the pitch was covered in snow when the players arrived. This and subsequent games had Foster quietly learning his trade, though there were worrying signs that he was physically 'off colour' more than a 20-year-old should have been. He did enjoy one great afternoon, however. At Leamington against Hants he enlivened the last overs of a draw with 51 not out in 30 minutes, the quickest-ever half-century for the county to date, and including two sixes and seven fours. (Foster himself beat the record, twice, in 1914.) He and Jim ('Tiger') Smith added 61 for the last wicket – the Tiger's share being six. It was the county's best last-wicket stand in a home game at the time. Two days later came the match of the season – the Australian tourists. The county was quite overmatched, only rain saving them from a heavy defeat. Foster was bowled for low scores and sent down 37 overs for 104 runs and one wicket. But what a wicket! He bowled the great Victor Trumper for a single.

A couple of weeks later, against Leicestershire, Foster enjoyed an even more memorable feat – with the bat. The match had started none too enjoyably for Foster, Warwicks and the home spectators. Albert Knight got his head down and stuck around for six and a half hours. He made 137, with only six fours and, remarkably 62 singles, and in one 45-minute spell obtained a mere single. Knight, deeply religious, reputedly said a prayer before his first ball and one imagines both opposition and spectators prayed for divine intervention long before their final deliverance. Foster came through his travails reasonably well, 28 overs bringing 73 runs and two wickets. First victim was John King, another renowned more for perspiration than inspiration. He and Knight had already ground out 45 together, 'sedately' according to Unite Jones in the local press. A long stand

29   R.S.Everitt, scion of a well known Black Country family, had played once for Worcestershire in 1901, and this was his sole Warwicks appearance. Surviving until 1973 he had time enough to cogitate upon his first-class career.

would have been almost more than humanity, or the average Rea Bank spectator could have stood. One hopes they thanked Foster. Fortunately after a first-innings collapse Quaife gave evidence of his own adhesive qualities. Quaife finished with an unbeaten century in five hours and actually outdid Knight, reaching the boundary only four times, but the star turn was young Frank Foster. He joined Quaife at 163 for five, his side still not out of the woods. Eighty minutes later they were safe. Foster raced to 51 out of 75 in 45 minutes and carried on to 97 out of 136 added with Quaife in 80 minutes. Sadly he was robbed of a glorious maiden century when he went down the wicket to the slow, innocuous and negative C.J.B.Wood and was bowled leg stump. According to Foster, Wood apologised for dismissing him with the worst ball of the innings. Disappointing end notwithstanding, any doubts about Foster were now gone and he had enabled his side to draw a game seemingly lost.

As the Warwicks season went into decline – twelfth position was not good enough and spelled the end of A.C.S.Glover's captaincy[30] – Foster too seemed to lose form. He and his colleagues received a dreadful hammering from local rivals Worcestershire, for whom Ted Arnold and W.B.Burns added 393 for the fifth wicket, still the best partnership in any Worcestershire match, and the best against Warwicks by any team until 2000. Worcestershire declared at 578 for six and inflicted upon Warwicks their heaviest ever defeat at Edgbaston – an innings and 233. Foster stuck to his task, figures of two for 115 in 47.1 overs comparing favourably with those of his team mates.

Foster regained form in the next match, innings figures of six for 46 against lowly Gloucestershire, but achieved little else of note on the first-class scene. After this game he went up to Pontefract visiting his Rowbotham relations and maybe the Foster Brothers shop. For Pontefract against Castleford he scored 173 not out in 90 minutes, his 35 fours including nine in succession. He also took four for 40 in a total of 150. Pontefract must have desired further visits while one wonders whether Yorkshire officials heard the news and rued the day William Foster decided to travel south to seek his fortune. On the first-class circuit Foster's season had become demonstrably stale, but he was after all only 20. His batting had improved remarkably; he achieved 541 runs at an average of 22.54, with three half-centuries all in quick time. His 49 wickets at 27.67 may seem unimpressive in generally favourable conditions, but he was inexperienced, not yet of man's estate and a reading of the reports suggests the seasoned professionals were usually given first chance though not always taking proper advantage. The Warwicks committee had now become well aware here was a jewel in their midst. But how to keep him?

Already Foster had hinted he owed himself first and foremost to business and spring 1910 saw matters become more urgent. He had met a girl, fallen

---

30   Alfred Glover, a useful batsman but undistinguished captain, was fortunate in
      never having to work, though he suffered severely reduced circumstances in
      later life.

in love, and wanted to marry her, so was giving up county cricket to devote himself to the hosiery trade. The committee was stunned, his father dismayed, county secretary R.V.Ryder typically pragmatic. He reckoned that whereas persuasion might fail, money could talk. After all Frank Foster was 'nearly' a Yorkshireman. Ryder was correct in his surmise. Dangling a £400 cheque he inveigled Frank into agreeing to sign as a professional for 1910. Old father William was appalled; no son of his was going to be a professional cricketer. He got together with C.S.Riddell and came to an agreement that Frank would play full-time for the county, returning to Wilkinson and Riddell off season all for an annual salary of £500. The deal was settled in Cabbie Williams' hansom taking Riddell to his fine house in Homer Road, Solihull. Actually before long the original reason for Foster's wishing to retire became invalid. The girl jilted him! Otherwise Frank would be starting the 1910 season in good order, his immediate financial future assured, and plenty more fish in the sea for a handsome young sportsman. Another problem was solved for Warwicks when Harold Goodwin, son of the county treasurer, Cambridge Blue and estimable allrounder, offered himself as captain, though pointing out he would not always be free to play. The committee decided they would use other amateurs when Goodwin felt unable to turn out; this slapdash way of doing things meant that, for three matches, Frank Foster was given the chance to see how he made out, so Goodwin's lack of commitment had its upside.

The 1910 season started miserably, with a two-day innings defeat away to Surrey. Foster took two wickets but swatted around inconclusively for 16 in each innings. The next game, with Lancashire, was cancelled due to the King's death, a strange decision since he could hardly be brought back to life, while a few hours watching Quaife, Kinneir and Baker putting bat to ball, or not, could have put spectators in a suitably sombre frame of mind. Normality restored, Warwicks went to New Road, Fred Bowley scored 118 on the first morning and he and Fred Pearson took the opening stand to 249 by 3 o'clock. Worcestershire reached 441 and still managed to get 30 minutes at the visitors. Foster's bowling stood out among the wreckage; in 24 overs, more than anyone else, he took five for 95. Skipper Goodwin sportingly brought himself on against the tail and took the last two for 19 in 6.4 overs. Fortunately rain gave Warwicks a draw. Northamptonshire at Edgbaston was limited to two days owing to the funeral of the King. Foster took seven cheap wickets but what with bad weather and funerals there was insufficient time to get a result. Poor weather, indifferent play and the lack of a regular captain saw Warwicks end May without even the sniff of a victory but Foster had bowled superbly, taking at least two wickets in every innings. His six for 58 against Sussex at Leamington, with little support, was an outstanding performance and deserved more than a draw. Three more 'five-fors' in June confirmed his bowling improvement but not until the end of the month did he register his first half-century. There was a 'match and a half' against Derbyshire at Blackwell Colliery. Derbyshire began day three needing nearly 200 to avoid an innings defeat. Assuming the match was as good as over the visiting pros went on a drinking spree –

but not only the pros. Foster himself reflected, '... the captain Joe Phillips and I were instrumental in throwing the game away. When had we gone to bed early, the match had been won.'

Foster figured on cigarette cards soon after the start of his career.

Initially the heroic drinking seemed to have had no effect. Eight wickets fell for 80 well before lunch. When John Chapman joined injured pace man Arnold Warren, 111 runs were still needed to make Warwicks bat again, the wicket was wearing, yet by lunch the deficit was only 33. Derbyshire secretary W.T.Taylor informed county historian Frank Peach years later that, during the interval, Frank Field was already showing signs of anxiety. 'Well Frank, you look like catching your early train,' said Taylor to Field, whose reply was 'I don't know, Mr Taylor, these chaps are pretty good bats,' and this day they certainly were. As the score mounted matters became stressful and theatrical. With Warren on 50, Foster, bowling fast leg-theory hit him sharply on the back of the knee at which Warren went down the wicket and threatened to hit Foster 'on the bloody head' if he didn't stop. But, though in pain, Warren continued scoring. At the other end Chapman, a slight man with an apologetic air, dominated proceedings and once hit Quaife onto adjoining allotments. The pair finally added 283, in just over three hours, still a world ninth-wicket record. Warren scored 123, Chapman went on to 165 before being bowled by Foster, and Derbyshire's all-out 430 meant Warwicks could only play out time. Foster, perhaps still hung over, bowled 26.4 overs for 119 runs and three wickets, and Field and Santall also did their stint. Phillips bowled only nine overs for 37, Quaife and Charlesworth bowled little. Poor, unimaginative, or hungover captaincy.

The county season continued on its undistinguished way, with the captaincy stakes now being joined by Lt Cowan. Hampshire's J.G.Greig put the bowlers to the sword – this future Catholic priest showed little mercy – but Foster played his part in the draw with 56 in 55 minutes. There followed a short break from the county scene. Foster showed he had been noted in high places and he was selected for the Gentlemen for their games at The Oval and Lord's, the highlights of a non-Test match season. The youngest participant in both games did little with the bat, but two innings analyses of four for 34 suggested genuine quality and Hamish Stuart in *Cricket* magazine proffered the view that 'F.R .Foster ... showed that he has the qualities which make for greatness.'

He could have been grateful to miss the Hampshire return, which saw an innings defeat. Goodwin, as near to being a non-playing captain as made no difference, bagged a 'pair' and bowled seven unproductive overs. The amateur contribution to this game makes interesting reading: W.H.Holbech achieved a 'pair' in his only first-class match and Collin Langley one and seven, and one for 40 in nine overs.

Warwicks now travelled up to the well-appointed Fartown ground, Huddersfield. An all-professional Yorkshire were led by a recently resurgent George Hirst. More significant was that for the first time Warwicks skipper was Frank Foster, at 21 the youngest ever, both before and since. For two days his side performed reasonably well but when set 266 in three hours they gave a deplorable display, all out 93. A first-innings 53 and match figures of five for 133 were reasonable but Foster gained few marks when being stumped for 17 'down the pitch'. The aim should have been a fighting draw.

For the remainder of the season Foster continued to bowl well, reaching his peak in the Derbyshire return in August. Fred Byrne, the season's fifth captain – a state of affairs that could not continue – batted and a score of 279 looked good when the visitors slumped to 120 for nine against some inspired bowling by Foster. A last-wicket stand of 87 between ex-Warwicks man Tom Forester and Joe Humphries improved matters but Foster's six wickets (five bowled) for 65 in 31 overs put his side in the driving seat. In the second innings he again bowled brilliantly, his six for 51 (four bowled) won the game and he became (and remains) the youngest to take ten in a match for the county.

Not that his bowling alone caught the eye. Against Surrey in Quaife's benefit match he top-scored in both innings, 77 in 110 minutes and 68 in 100 minutes. He seemed on course for a maiden century but in the second innings he got himself out. The reason? He had arranged to go to Prestatyn with his parents to see a girl with whom he fancied himself to be in love. Warwicks succumbed by 42 runs. *Cricket* magazine said: ' ... it is to be hoped he will not allow his batting to develop at the expense of his bowling. Only in comparatively few instances has a cricketer proved a mainstay ... with both bat and ball and it is noticeable that in the match wherein Foster scored so well he took only three wickets at a cost of nearly 32 each.'

In the last match, Lancashire at Blackpool, with Foster as skipper, Warwicks had the best of things before poor weather ensured a draw. More pertinently, when dismissing Jack Sharp – the third of four second-innings victims – he completed 100 for the season. He remains the youngest Warwicks bowler to perform the feat. His season ended quietly with two games in the Scarborough Festival and an appearance for The Rest *v* Kent, the county champions, at The Oval. But 112 wickets, at an average of 21.19, in 24 matches: what a record for a 21-year-old!

Chapter Five

Tell Kent from me she hath lost

Founded in 1882, Warwicks were elected to the County Championship in 1895 but had since hovered anonymously around mid-table, with teams comprised of under-achieving professionals and various dilettante amateurs. In 1910 they drifted to fourteenth, only Derbyshire and Somerset below them. Worse, the previous four seasons local rivals, Worcestershire, finished higher. It seemed out of the question that a challenge could be mounted to the old counties. Kent, Middlesex and Surrey in the south, Lancashire, Nottinghamshire and Yorkshire up north seemed resentful of the Midland interlopers – why else the reluctance to arrange fixtures? Middlesex and Notts had never yet played the Edgbaston side in the Championship while Kent had not done so since 1899. Kent had won successive titles – perhaps it's easier if one is allowed to pick and choose opponents. In the circumstances Warwicks did not expect too

The Warwickshire side pictured early in the 1911 season.
Standing (l to r): Richards (trainer), E.J.Smith (wk), J.H.Parsons, C.Charlesworth, S.Kinneir.
Seated: S.Santall, F.G.Stephens, F.R.Foster (capt), G.W.Stephens, E.F.Field.
On the ground: W.G.Quaife, C.S.Baker.

much, but were anxious for some progress. Perhaps with a touch of desperation they turned to 21-year-old Frank Foster but, to their dismay, after accepting the offer in January he changed his mind, announcing his retirement for the second time.

Perhaps the club should not have been surprised; he had regularly hinted that each season would be his last. Spring 1911 was different however; he had fallen in love (again), wished to announce his engagement and wanted to concentrate on work.

Frank quit so late the county was in a quandary, turning to Lt Charles Cowan to lead them in the opening game, against Surrey, 1910 runners-up with a phalanx of top professionals led by those gifts to their working class supporters, 'ayward, 'obbs, 'ayes and 'Bl'itch'. Cowan, a naval type whose most valuable work was as a future committeeman and honorary treasurer, was keen but short on ability, and his performance here also suggests a chronic lack of leadership qualities. All out for 62 and 87, Warwicks were hopelessly beaten by an innings. The only pieces of encouragement were the efforts of young professionals Harold Bates and Jack Parsons.[31]

Warwicks were in trouble, not least from the London press, especially in the form of E.H.D.Sewell who airily announced they were 'not even a good second-eleven side'. As soon as the defeat was telegraphed to R.V.Ryder, the wires began humming. Ryder to William Foster, and a plea to persuade his son to change his mind and come to the rescue of Warwicks cricket. Off went William to Wilkinson and Riddell, to persuade his talented but maverick son his county needed him: 'They want you, my boy; you had better go.' Fresh financial arrangements were made and the saviour of Warwicks raced to the rescue, perhaps not on a white charger, more likely in a carriage pulled by one of father's hacks.

Dressing-room reaction[32] was mixed but Foster addressed his players and stressed his belief in the team ethic – 'all for one, one for all' – but this message seemed to collapse in a heap when, for Foster's debut at Old Trafford, he and Lt Cowan travelled first-class, the professionals third-class. Perhaps change needed to come by degrees; after all he had a pretty disparate group under him – a full gamut of post-Edwardian England in fact. His squad included businessmen, a Naval officer, a resentful ex-Test player, a stockbroker, a solicitor, a type two syphilid, an England-class boozer, an ex-farm labourer, a professional who once played

---

31 Harold Bates, son of groundsman Jack Bates was a promising pace bowler killed in the war. Brother Len became a county stalwart however. Jack Parsons was a remarkable man, starting as a professional and finishing as a canon of the Church of England. His personality also metamorphosed: 'one of the lads', hard drinking and with an enviable range of 'Anglo-Saxon', became the intolerant puritan, while his style changed from stodgy defence to free hitting. He was one of few batsmen – the last was E.R.Dexter in the 1962 Test – to hit a ball clean over the old Edgbaston pavilion into the road.

32 More accurately dressing *rooms*, since facilities were still divided between amateurs and professionals.

violin in Manchester children's orchestra and the groundsman's son. Foster needed to get them pulling in the same direction.

Foster's other message was to play positively. 'Always attack' was a motto he adhered to all his life and he was ever-critical of those players guilty of what he regarded as too much caution, which he felt was allied to on-field selfishness. He reckoned 'The bat should always beat the hands of the clock. By that I mean at least sixty-one runs an hour and, if both batsmen at the wicket cannot manage that between them, it is a sorry look out for the poor spectator and for the advance of brighter cricket.'

For the most part Foster's ideas struck a chord with the professionals, with one sad exception. Arthur Frederick Augustus Lilley, known as 'Dick', was now 44, a veteran of 35 Tests, and had played for the county before his new skipper was born. Sadly matters 'blew up' in mid-season.

The team for the Lancashire game was Foster, Lilley, Kinneir, Charlesworth, Quaife, Baker, Parsons, Lt Cowan, Santall, Tiger Smith, and Field. Two changes from The Oval side yet, in hindsight, not too bad a team on paper. Foster needed to convert paper theory to on-field effectiveness, and how he was to succeed!

Foster won the toss and elected to bat, sending in Lilley and Sep Kinneir to launch a new era. Three wickets had fallen for 79 when down the pavilion steps swaggered the new skipper, no doubt wearing his trademark white muffler and eager to make an impression. A minute or so later he was walking back whence he came. Maybe he tried to force the pace too soon, or Jimmy Heap beat him in flight, or spun the ball more, or less, than expected. Whatever the cause Foster was bowled first ball. What a start! There was then a slump to 91 for six, but welcome succour came from an unlikely place. Lt Cowan, villain of the Surrey debacle, and a couple of tailenders took the score to 201, Cowan's share an unbeaten 51. Cowan had progressed to Captain, and a war had intervened before posting his second half-century, but clearly he was no complete duffer.

Despite his inauspicious start with the bat Foster led his men out for the first time with head unbowed and Lancashire were soon 13 for two. Unfortunately Lancashire's No.3, Johnny Tyldesley, was still there and his record against Warwicks was awesome – 2,627 runs, ten centuries, average of 75.05. So, what did the skipper do? Let Foster himself take up the story:

> When Tyldesley came in first wicket down I, like the fool I am, beckoned to Jack Parsons and requested him to take the next over. Dick Lilley exclaimed 'Great Scott! Are you mad?' In his first over Jack bowled the worst ball I have ever seen, a yard outside Johnny's leg stump. What did Johnny do? He swung his bat round with his left hand only, as much as if to say 'this ball is no good' the ball hit the edge of the bat, went up into the air, and 'Tiger' Smith caught Johnny out at 13.

Foster's crazy switch had paid off and with his first ball Parsons had dismissed one of England's greatest with a crass long hop. 'Take him off now!' yelled the nonplussed Lilley, who seemed to think Foster was making a mockery of the game. Warwicks gained a lead of 46 and then Foster tried another unorthodox tactic, putting himself in first but this did not work; he was unable to get the medium-fast Harry Dean away and scored only four out of 21 before skying Dean for a catch in the deep. The rest, led by Charlesworth with 110, saw Lancashire requiring 416 for victory. They were in trouble almost from the outset and when John Tyldesley again failed – bowled on the back foot by a trimmer from Field – they must have known it was not their day. Lancashire lost by 137 runs, with the game ending in light-hearted farce when last men Lol Cook and Bill Worsley got themselves in a tangle attempting a quick single. (Surely a snatched run was hardly the most important requirement at this stage.)

On his debut as official skipper Foster had orchestrated Warwicks' best win for years, their first over Lancashire since 1902, something they did not repeat at Old Trafford until 1936, and the manner of its achieving could not be overstated. Just 22, he had galvanized team spirit, shown originality in thought, and the courage to implement his ideas. This success only served to reinforce some of his more unorthodox convictions. Tyldesley's dismissal by Parsons, for instance, strengthened Foster's quirky but fervent belief in the properties of the number 13.

Back-to-back home wins against Leicestershire and Sussex confirmed the 'Foster effect' and his own form seemed to be returning. His 34 against Sussex ended a run of seven single-figure scores for the county, while a first-innings spell of six for 40 laid the foundations for victory. Three wins on the bounce, and no doubt the new skipper was pleased as Punch. So too his Dad, having persuaded him to put cricket before commerce. The championship table now made interesting reading: Kent top, Yorkshire second, Surrey and Notts fourth and fifth. But sandwiched in the middle of this old guard gang of four was Frank Foster's Warwicks. The transformation had been noted and, in an interview for *Fry's Magazine*, he felt they had 'a good and enterprising side.' Warwickshire had been under-rated 'because the papers are so used to running our cricket down, they cannot get out of the groove.'

He later said: 'I carried with me a little book at each match. The maximum number of marks I gave a man for each match was five. A brilliant catch at a crucial moment may earn five marks, a great bit of stumping might do it, or a brilliant run out, or even twenty runs made quickly. Time is everything when a county eleven is trying to win every match. Warwickshire never played for a draw under my captaincy. Never once did I take notice of a big innings on a good wicket when that innings occupied too long a time.'

Foster's words regarding his philosophy as captain must have seemed like a shot across the bows to Kinneir, Quaife, Lilley and Baker, who could stonewall with the best of them, but though it was still early days, things looked promising. Matters were about to come down to earth with a bump.

Worcestershire at New Road, a local derby, but despite lacking all but one of their own Fosters,[33] the home side set the visitors 300 and won by 116 runs. Foster himself struggled with the ball and must have been annoyed at twice getting stumped off Simpson-Hayward's 'lobs'.[34] But Foster was just girding his loins; Yorkshire were next – a team of all the talents. Master bowlers Hirst and Rhodes were a little 'over the hill' but Major Booth and Alonzo Drake had added new depth to the attacking strength. Yorkshire were naturally led by an amateur, Everard Radcliffe, a Devonian not thought worth a Cambridge trial.

Warwicks batted but were five down for 61 when the captain joined Lilley. They set about the bowlers, especially Wilfred Rhodes, with such abandon they added 96 in 55 minutes and, after Lilley departed, Foster remained aggressively defiant in another fine stand, 97 with Santall, and when finally bowled by Drake had reached 105 – his maiden century – in 135 minutes, with a six and twelve fours. He had shown maturity in his best innings to date and saved his side from potential disaster. A total of 317 was not unsatisfactory.

Foster could not have wished for a better start when Yorkshire batted: the first ball of the innings whipped out Ben Wilson's middle stump. But then Rhodes and David Denton added 124 before Field dismissed the former for a typically gritty 47. Foster then had Denton taken at slip by Lilley but Hirst joined Drake and they added 152 for the fourth wicket before the most inspired spell thus far of Foster's career. Hirst had remarked to Tiger Smith that he couldn't understand how Foster got so many lbw decisions. Tiger told Foster, at which he brought himself back, at 299 for three. His first ball hit Hirst on his now ample posterior, and the second straightened from middle and leg to remove the off stump. He bowled Hirst, Drake and Turner in four balls and actually took the last seven wickets, six of them bowled, in 33 balls for 31 runs. Figures of 29.3 overs, four maidens, 118 runs, nine wickets, were to remain a career best but he must have been unimpressed at the poor support afforded by his professional colleagues which enabled Yorkshire to post a first-innings lead of 30. As disappointing must have been the second-innings batting. Only Kinneir of the seasoned professionals showed much backbone, though Foster would have been annoyed allowing himself to be stumped for the third time in four innings. Set 216, Yorkshire were guided home by Alonzo Drake, after Foster had briefly raised hopes with three more wickets. Foster had become only the second Warwicks player to hit a century and take ten wickets in a match. Quaife had done it against Worcestershire in 1901, and at least finished on the winning side. No-one has done it since. For his first-

---

33   The privileged sons of a local vicar, and not above bending the rules to suit their own particular brand of sportsmanship. Rumour has it that 'our' Foster was annoyed at the frequent assumption that he was related; his apparent feelings of contempt blew up in 1914 – as will be seen.

34   In the 1909/10 South African series George Simpson-Hayward was the last player chosen for Tests for his lob bowling. The tour captain was his relation, H.D.G.Leveson Gower – subsequently knighted 'for services to cricket'.

innings bowling Foster was presented with the ball and afterwards it was reported that he demonstrated to George Hirst how he obtained lbws, but a second successive defeat and the apparent lack of fight from some senior players must have concerned him.

Early June and the championship table had a familiar look, Warwicks having subsided to mid-table mediocrity. Surely the young captain would not be satisfied with this. There was now a short Championship break however, when the All-India touring team visited. They had not been given Test status and their performance explained why. The team was weakened by the absence of its best player, K.M.Mistry; contemporary reports state he was 'kept away by Coronation duties with the Maharaja of Patiala'. Strange priorities indeed.[35] Warwicks swept the tourists aside; Foster took seven wickets but the most impressive bowling came from another left-arm pace man Basil Crawford. Making his debut, Crawford took six for 36 in his first bowl, but never again approached such form.

Back to the Championship and a close game with Derbyshire at Blackwell. There were few early highlights on a poor wicket, but in the second innings, Foster decided conditions were against George Stephens' strong top-handed methods and deputed Tiger Smith to open with Kinneir. They added 67 and Smith eventually scored 81 in 150 minutes, 'worth 250 in good conditions' according to his skipper. Left to get 176 Derbyshire would have felt confident but on 41 for no wicket Sam Cadman was adjudged lbw by umpire 'Shoey' Harrison. When Foster pointed out that Cadman had edged the ball first Harrison brusquely told him to mind his own business. Cadman was forced to depart, his expression no doubt even more lugubrious than usual. Derbyshire edged forward however and with 40 needed, and four wickets left they may have fancied their chances. Foster had another ace to play however. In his own words: 'I said to Frank Field, who had been bowling awful rubbish, "Come off, Crawford bowls." Field replied, "Are you mad, skipper?" "Quite," I murmured. With the fifth ball of his second over Crawford bowled 'Nudger' Needham, with a long hop.' 'It was a rotten ball but a very important wicket,' recalled Foster. 'Crawford was a tall, lanky individual who tried to bowl fast. The ball he got Needham with pitched short and went straight for the head. Needham ducked, the ball hit his gloves and dropped onto the wickets.'

There was a bizarre ending. At 153 for eight, Humphries ran himself out and then the well-set skipper John Chapman saw last man Warren start for a run but, when sent back, the big paceman was too slow on the turn and failed to make his ground. The contemporary press blamed the two professionals (of course) for being bad judges of running but, whoever was at fault, Derbyshire had lost a match they might have expected to win. The run-outs sealed their fate, but Foster's master strokes of opening with Tiger and giving Crawford the ball created the opportunity.

---

35   For another, off-beat reason the absence of M.D.Bulsara from the Edgbaston match was a disappointment. The best-looking member of the party was reputedly a relation of rock musician Freddy Mercury.

The next game, at Gloucester, was lost disappointingly despite mighty efforts by Field, match figures of 12 for 79, and Foster missed the following game, with Hampshire. His form and flair had been noticed and he was chosen for England *v* The Rest at Lord's, a match billed as a Test trial despite there being no Test matches until the next winter.[36] It was a hotchpotch of a game, attracting little spectator interest. Hobbs, 'indisposed', did not play; Syd Barnes refused the invitation for no reason other than his being Barnes. The Rest batted and Foster soon dismissed Wally Hardinge, caught by Frank Tarrant.[37] There were two down at the break, P.F.Warner and Somerset's Talbot Lewis together. What Foster ate for luncheon is not known but in the afternoon he tore through the batting, dismissing Warner, J.W.Hearne, Hendren, Woolley, W.B.Burns and 'Razor' Smith in a superb spell of fast left-arm bowling. After lunch he took six wickets for 50, finishing with seven for 76 in 31.3 overs. The Rest were all out 173. England's reply of 393 owed much to a very slow stand of 170 between James Iremonger and Wilfred Rhodes. Both probably had their eyes on a winter tour place (they were picked) and with his bowling now very much disregarded at top level Rhodes knew runs were required. He made 121 but scored slower and slower, his last 21 taking an hour. No wonder that, when his turn at the wicket came around, Foster got himself stumped for eight. The Rest eventually saved the match in miserable weather before an equally miserable 'crowd' but Foster's first-day performance surely opened eyes at Lord's.

Meanwhile a Fosterless Warwicks, led by ex-skipper Fred Byrne, were laying waste to Hampshire, with Sep Kinneir[38] scoring an unbeaten 268 in seven hours, at the time the best by a Warwicks batsman, and the best by a left hander, an opener and at Edgbaston until 1994. Such was his dominance that Kinneir scored more runs in his one innings than Hants in both innings combined. Field recorded his only hat-trick in a stunning win by an innings and 296 runs. A delighted Foster, at the pavilion gate to welcome his victorious players would have had something to say to the team in general, Kinneir and Field in particular.

---

36   There had been an earlier Test trial, at Sheffield at the beginning of June, but Foster was not involved, even though Warwicks were without a match. So his form had only just started to attract attention.

37   A peculiar choice for an 'England' side since as an Australian professional he was not thought to be qualified. At the time Tarrant was arguably the best all-rounder in the world and really should have 'walked' into the England eleven.

38   Kinneir, aged 40, became Foster's staunchest supporter. His own life had been fraught by tragedy and disappointment. The seventh son in a Corsham, Wiltshire family, he qualified in 1898, played promisingly but then 'disappeared' until late in the 1899 season. Only years later did he confide in Frank Foster. Though already 27 he knew little of life and at Cheltenham for the Gloucestershire game he met and fell in love with what he described as 'an exquisite young girl'. He fell ill and the club sent him to Germany for treatment. When he returned his hair had gone, his finger nails turned blue and fell out. Syphilis was the problem and fortunately it was caught before his brain was affected but his life was changed for ever, and he never again trusted a woman. In view of Foster's subsequent health problems maybe there was more to this story, told by Foster in the 1930s, than meets the eye.

Table-topping Surrey were next at Edgbaston but Foster cared little for reputations and totally stole the show on day one. Going in at 124 for three he went on to a marvellous 200 out of 307 in three hours, with three sixes and 21 fours. Contemporary reports say he drove with supreme power and authority and was particularly severe on Surrey's best bowler, Hitch. His fifty came up in 45 minutes, 100 in 100 minutes and 150 in 140 minutes. He added 125 for the fourth wicket with Parsons, 151 for the fifth with Lilley. He was finally caught by Hobbs chancing his arm against occasional bowler W.A.Spring. There was only one bit of luck; he called Parsons for an 'impossible' single, Hobbs threw the ball in but it struck a bowler's footmark, evaded Strudwick and went for four overthrows. Warwicks were all out 501 just before the close. Next day Surrey struggled to 182 for nine before a stand of 130 between Hitch, whose 82 occupied 62 minutes and Strudwick took them to respectability. Foster batted again and Kinneir and Tiger Smith answered his call for quick runs, adding 176 in 135 minutes, Smith achieving a maiden century, and Foster asked Surrey to score 396. The track was good but fine bowling by Field seemed to be sending his side to victory at eight down for 187. Unfortunately Ernest Hayes, who scored a hundred, after annoying Foster and his men by refusing to 'walk' when caught at slip, was joined by Rushby and an unbeaten stand of 82 saw the game saved. 'Atrocious luck,' pleaded Foster, but really an inability to wheedle out tailenders was the problem. Warwicks remained mid-table but Foster was into his batting stride; the fuse had been lit.

Meanwhile a break from the county scene. The Gentlemen met the Players at The Oval, then Lord's. Foster was picked for the former each time, but slightly surprising were Kinneir's selection for The Oval, and Tiger Smith for Lord's. Manifestly, despite their side's inconsistency, their play had been noted, and there was a party for Australia to be selected.

The Gentlemen won the toss at The Oval and their innings of 466 was dominated by a superb 190 in five hours by Lancastrian R.H.Spooner, but Foster at No.8, dominated a seventh-wicket stand of 64 in 35 minutes with Kent's A.P.Day; Foster's share was 40. The Players' innings was a personal triumph for Kinneir; perhaps sensing the possibility of a belated overseas tour he batted nearly five and a half hours for a magnificent 158. The highlight was a stand of 145 in two hours with George Gunn. Maybe the dour, taciturn Sep permitted himself a satisfied smile, perhaps removing his cap to give the spectators a sight of his bald pate and even downing a quick half – of shandy of course – later. Foster took only two wickets but would certainly have been delighted for Kinneir.

Foster then crossed the Thames, making for Lord's for the second of the season's matches of a series that had epitomised cricket's social divide since 1806. Quite what Tiger Smith, working-class Brummie from Benacre Street, Highgate, thought of it all is unknown but he would have been delighted to represent the Players opposing his county skipper. The Gents put on a solid show but Foster, from No.8, alone attempted to 'get after' Syd Barnes, who had dismissed five of the best batsmen. Foster monopolized a stand of 72 with Johnny Douglas and scored 65 in an hour. All that the magazine *Cricket* had to say was that he brought off some 'capital hits'. The Players were restricted to 201 and Foster dismissed Hobbs, Rhodes and Hirst but the wicket that gave him most pleasure was 'Tiger' Smith's, such was his quirky way. Foster scored an aggressive 32 second knock and though his two second-innings wickets cost 93 he played his part in the Gentlemen's victory, and would have returned to Edgbaston to take on Northamptonshire with a spring in his step.

Warwicks made a scrappy start. Foster himself scored 24 out of 31 added for the fourth wicket with Quaife. He had just hit six and four in successive balls but then clattered the inoffensive leg spin of John Denton down the throat of Bob Haywood. Fortunately Quaife dominated the remainder of the innings; he 'farmed' the later bowling so expertly he actually scored 113 in only 150 minutes. A total of 267 began to look good when Northamptonshire found themselves on 57 for six and then 121 for nine but, inspired by a century by West Indian Syd Smith, they reached 189 before Foster bowled wicket-keeper Buswell. A lead of 78 looked good but Warwicks had lost three for 32 when Foster joined Quaife. They added 123, Foster's share a blistering 98 in 90 minutes with ten fours and a six before he went down the wicket to Syd Smith and was stumped by the portly, but agile Walter Buswell. Northamptonshire finally needed 309 but collapsed so abjectly they were soon 36 for six and eventually all out 81. Foster added five for 25 to his first innings four for 79 and scored 24 and 98. For the second time in the season he had scored 100 runs and taken eight wickets in a match. He was to perform this feat four times in all. In the whole history of Warwicks cricket six players have achieved such an allround performance, Foster alone more than once.

Travelling next to Chichester in Sussex, Foster won the toss for the ninth championship game in succession and Warwicks achieved their first 'double' of the season owing a huge debt to Kinneir, who became the first to record a century in each innings for the county. Foster supported him well second knock with 65 at a run a minute; then his five for 52 saw them home.

Back to Edgbaston and the Gloucestershire match had more than usual interest, with a Saturday start for the first time. A first-day crowd of some 12,000 suggested the experiment was a success. The visitors won the toss and reached 340. Foster had another 'five-for' and Field dismissed the dangerously adhesive Charles Barnett and the more aggressive G.L.Jessop. Warwicks made a consistent reply; Foster hit 56 in 45 minutes but the backbone was another Quaife century. Gloucestershire did enough to set Warwicks a target of 149 on the third afternoon but any worries were quickly forgotten. Going in at three, Foster played like a man inspired. His 87 in 75 minutes with two sixes, set them on their way and after he was bowled by the persevering youngster Dipper, only 20 were required. Yet another match where Foster achieved the rare 100 runs and eight wickets feat. His 143 runs took a mere 120 minutes, while accurate leg-theory brought eight for 135 in 47.2 overs. Another extraordinary, match-winning performance.

The Gloucestershire win was meritorious but the Yorkshire return, at Harrogate, was more memorable, yet tinged with sadness. Warwicks had bested the Tykes only once in 35 matches but a win here, however unlikely, would put them among the championship leaders. The team arrived about 10 am on the first morning and a Yorkshire committee man asked Foster if he would object to a new wicket being cut, the original one being off-centre. Lilley said that Yorkshire had no bowler as quick as Field and as the new wicket was dry and hard, 'win the toss and you've won the match'. He also said that a new wicket was hardly likely to last three days. Foster did win the toss and gratefully elected to bat, much to the disappointment of Sir Archibald White, another of the aristocratic skippers preferred by Yorkshire. Charlesworth, with 93, was the main contributor to the Warwicks total of 341, but the fireworks were supplied by Foster, whose 60 in a fourth-wicket stand of 75 with Quaife took only 40 minutes. Foster and Field took early Yorkshire wickets but fine batting by Drake, with 99, and Hirst resulted in a recovery that took Yorks to within 31 of the visitors. Warwicks soon lost three wickets in their second innings but then Foster played another captain's innings. According to F.G.Stephens' memoirs it was his best ever. His 101 in 105 minutes took his match total to 161 in 145 minutes, with four sixes. He had now hit five successive half-centuries, a Warwicks record until beaten by Fred Gardner in 1950, and all Foster's innings had come at a run a minute or more. Requiring 257 the home side made the 'best' of the worn wicket and surrendered themselves abjectly for 56 all out. Field was brilliant, achieving an analysis of seven for 20. This was a fourth successive victory; Warwicks were now third with Notts, and leaders Kent firmly in their sights. As for Foster, there was surely no more devastating an allrounder in world cricket. It was not yet the end of July but he had already passed 1,000 runs and was approaching the 'double'.

This match was full of incident apart from the win. Repeatedly hit on the thigh by Foster, George Hirst threatened to throw his bat at the bowler, while on the second night, with Yorks already one for 14, Foster requested the wicket be guarded against overnight 'watering' by over-protective home supporters. It was later reckoned it had been doctored, but some good it did Yorkshire. Foster had then gone for a 'hectic' night out with friends, and maybe relations, from Huddersfield and only tumbled into bed about an hour before Field woke him at 7 am, with the news that he was about to have a cold bath and massage. Despite protests Field picked him up and carried him to the bathroom where the trainer ran the tap and Foster reckoned that for an hour he was 'thumped and bumped, bounced and bashed, rubbed and dubbed' and then given a steak and a can of beer. Play then started and Field immediately had Rhodes caught – by Foster. 'How do you feel, skip?' asked the 'kindly' Field. 'Go to the devil' was the friendly reply.

These events had happy endings; but as we have said, there was also some sadness. Lilley had always had trouble taking Foster. His hands and fingers had been knocked about, but Foster's deceptive pace off the pitch from leg also caused problems. So Tiger Smith had taken over the gloves, with Lilley playing as a batsman but unhappy serving under Foster. During the second morning Lilley, from short leg, started waving his arms about, directing fielders. Lilley knew of Denton's penchant for the lofted drive and so felt some of the fielders should be deeper. Unfortunately instead of telling Foster he moved the fielders himself, his voice loud enough to be heard by spectators. Foster reminded him, also loudly, that he – not Lilley – was captain, and if Lilley had any advice to offer he should just tell him. 'Don't make me look a fool,' he told Lilley, at which Lilley walked into the long field where he remained until lunch. After the interval Foster went into the professionals' room and was apparently greeted with dead silence, and no-one spoke as he led them onto the field. Things remained low key for the remainder of Yorkshire's innings but during Foster's brilliant century Lilley, batting opposite, came up and congratulated him on his batting. 'It was the best I have seen, and I've seen them all'. Such obsequiousness was most unlike Lilley.

That evening one of the professionals told Foster that during lunch Lilley had tried to persuade the rest of the players not to take the field after the interval. He complained he had never been spoken to in the way Foster had spoken that morning, and he wasn't going to stand 'a young kid of 22' telling him what to do. The others gave Lilley's strike call short shrift and had Field not injured his elbow Lilley may not have played in the next match. But, travelling straight to Southampton with no spare man, there was little choice but to include him. When, however, on the Sunday before the next home game, with Worcestershire, R.V.Ryder telephoned to ask who he wanted in the team, Foster replied, 'There is one I do not want to play: Dick Lilley.'

The Hampshire match, with Field absent and a 'feeling' between Foster and Lilley, proved an anti-climax after Harrogate, a last-wicket stand of 88 between young Alec Kennedy and Eric Olivier, a Cambridge Blue, propelling Hampshire to 283. Foster seemed off colour but did take three wickets to complete his 'double' for the season. Another fine innings by Kinneir – his 148 was reported as 'chanceless' – helped towards to a good lead but Warwicks' optimism may have been tempered by the knowledge that Southampton wickets usually lasted, and Hampshire, in this dry, sunny season, had exceeded 400 in every match but one. Phil Mead and A.C.Johnston put on 292 for the third wicket (still the county's record against Warwicks), destroying all hopes of another victory and when Hampshire declared on 457 Mead was unbeaten on 207, his first double century, taking only three hours. Foster seemed distracted, conceding 75 in 17 overs and opening the second innings swished around wildly to score the first ten runs before succumbing. Despite the draw Warwicks retained third spot. The conversation with Ryder confirmed Foster had another matter on his mind – the problem of Lilley, unsympathetic excess baggage who must not be allowed to spoil what Foster had built up. Foster had his way and Lilley was omitted for the Worcestershire game. Perhaps the skipper had been cruel, but maybe there was also kindness in his action. Lilley never played again.

The Worcestershire match was played in extreme heat. Batting first, Warwicks played indifferently but their innings was rescued by a fourth-wicket stand of 112 between Quaife and Foster, who again played brilliantly hitting 85 in 90 minutes. A total of 274 began to look good when Foster took four of the first five wickets for 45, his victims including Geoffrey and Harry of the 'other' Fosters, but the Worcestershire later order rallied to 193. Fine knocks by Frank Stephens and Baker (the latter replacing Lilley) and a typically aggressive 62 in 55 minutes from Foster enabled Warwicks to set 466 for victory on the final day. Field left the field with sunstroke and a stand of 156 between Arnold and W.B.Burns seemed to put victory beyond reach. When Foster belatedly brought himself back at 301 for seven and bowled Burrows they had a whiff of hope but Burns and Simpson-Hayward stood firm until stumps. Had Foster declared earlier the result may have been different but Field was unwell and the veterans Quaife and Santall also faltered in the heat. Third spot was maintained however, though no ground was made up on Kent or Middlesex.

Next day saw lowly Derbyshire at Edgbaston. The match had to be won to rekindle the flagging title chase, but ex-Warwicks man Forester found a bumpy pitch helped him and 170 all out began to look even worse when Cadman and John Chapman – ever a thorn in the Bears' flesh, or perhaps it should be paw – raced to 149 for one. With Field and Foster then extracting the sort of life found by Forester there was a collapse to 238 all out, Field five for 96, Foster four for 66. Warwicks made another sticky start but, as ever, the skipper responded with 70 in 70 minutes. Quaife achieved a more staid century and an hour into the last day Derbyshire were given a victory target of 346, a hard task soon rendered hopeless. Sensing a return to winning ways Foster took the first six wickets and had a spell of four for eight in an hour. He then tired but he had done the damage and the visitors subsided to a 165-run defeat. Foster's six for 37 gave him a match return of ten for 103 in 46.4 overs, while his second-innings aggression kick-started the march to victory. Was there nothing he, and through him, his team, could not now achieve?

Lancashire, having just done Warwicks a favour by beating Kent were next visitors to Edgbaston. Any disappointment at losing the toss disappeared as Field and Foster consigned Lancashire to 50 for four. Ernest Tyldesley battled hard for 71 in two hours but no-one stayed with him, there being no fifty partnerships in their 210. Field, again in fine form, had five for 78. Warwicks started badly but Kinneir and Quaife played so well that by the close the arrears were only 33, with eight wickets left. After a mini-collapse next morning, Foster and George Stephens then added 123 for the seventh wicket in fine style. They batted only 60 minutes before Foster, on 98 at one-a-minute, was unluckily bowled by a Jack Sharp 'shooter'. No matter, Warwicks went on to 422, and a lead of 212.

With nearly a day and a half left, Lancashire would have hoped to aim for a safe target and at 141 for two, with John Tyldesley and Sharp going well. Perhaps they would have been optimistic. A fighting draw seemed a distinct possibility; however, that 141 for two in late afternoon became 172 all out next morning, seven of the last eight wickets falling to Field, during which time he conceded only 12 runs. In another fantastic performance Warwicks had destroyed a team on the fringe of the title race and confirmed, beyond doubt, their title credentials.

Team and supporters would have left Edgbaston after the season's final home match light of heart and step. For the first time since May they had an average of more than 70% of points taken against points possible. Victory in their final two matches – both away, though Leicestershire and Northamptonshire were hardly the stiffest opposition – and long-time leaders Kent needed to win three of their last four games and remain unbeaten, as did Middlesex should Kent falter. Already the whinges were being dusted off. 'The fixture list was unfair', yet had the southern counties wished to play Warwicks they could have done so. In addition more interest should have been shown in trying to ensure all counties played each other.

So, Leicestershire at Hinckley; another Saturday start and Warwicks' first first-class game in Leicestershire outside the county town. For those interested in irrelevancies the first match played by a team styling itself 'Warwickshire' was against 'Leicestershire' on Gosford Green, Coventry some 68 years earlier almost to the day. 'Warwickshire' won that one; victory this time would be somewhat sweeter. Warwicks won the toss and went off like an express train. Smith and Kinneir batted well but the innings really took off when Foster joined Charlesworth and scored 40 of a stand of 72 in 35 minutes. Charlesworth, 142 out of 255 in 150 minutes, played a massive part in his side's all out 365. The strong position was confirmed when Foster (four for 57) and Field (six for 83) were the main architects of Leicestershire's all out 164. One bright spot for the home team was C.J.B.Wood's unbeaten 54, which meant his carrying his bat through the innings for a record thirteenth time, and the fifth time in 1911 alone. He didn't win many matches but certainly stayed there. Possibly the only other thing Wood took out of the match was commercial; Wood was a coal merchant and Joe Phillips, a surprise choice for the visitors, contributed little to the cricket, but he managed a nearby colliery.

Leicestershire followed on and again failed dismally. Only a third-wicket stand of 50 between Harry Whitehead, a fine batsman but consistent underperformer and Cecil Boden, an amateur whose cricket was nipped in the bud by his entering the Church,[39] detained Foster's men for long and

---

39   Rev Cecil Boden's performances suggest he made the right decision to take
      Holy Orders. In eleven first-class matches for Leicestershire, spread over three
      seasons, he scored 196 runs at 10.31. Living until 1981 he had ample time to
      reflect on the matter.

Leicestershire lost by an innings in under two days. It was a happy band of cricketers who went off to Northampton; Warwicks' triumph there is fully covered in Foster's own words in Chapter One.

Warwicks' success had already begun to grip the imagination in some quarters. Headed 'F.R.Foster – An Appreciation', appeared in *Cricket* magazine, page 473, a poem to her hero penned by Phyllis Jeanie Rickards:

> Warwick, your day has dawned at last,
> You've found a leader, born and bred,
> The wooden spoon for you has past
> Now Foster's head.
>
> See how his fighting power resists,
> And plucketh out the stagnant weeds.
> Who would refuse to join the lists?
> When Foster leads.
>
> From the pavilion, to and fro,
> A long and sad procession strolls;
> There's not much chance for them you know,
> When Foster bowls.
>
> No chance for that poor chap who skies;
> The fiercest drive a single yields;
> Its energy personified
> When Foster fields.
>
> The score mounts up by leap and bound,
> The bowlers try a swerve of spin,
> But boundaries are always found
> When Foster's in.
>
> The scorer sharpens up his point,
> And point he sharpens up his wits,
> For soon the bowling's out of joint
> When Foster hits.
>
> England is rich with such a man,
> And Warwick you are richer still,
> You'll never be an 'also-ran'
> With Foster's skill.
>
> The team rejoice in life renewed,
> The fairest flower they bring to grief;
> They fight and win the fiercest feud
> When Foster's chief.
>
> Warwick, good luck, don't rest content
> Until you win and fame renowned
> Succeed in leading Midds and Kent
> Then Foster's crowned.

No poetry prizes, but from the heart. Whether Foster saw these words before the last match is impossible to say, nor would one know whether he took the comments on board, but whatever their pertinence to the situation, he had a title to win. And this he did!

The day after the Northamptonshire match, *The Birmingham Post* described the game and the team's arrival in Birmingham. It also had its man[40] at the Grand Hotel reception: 'Thousands of people had assembled along the route, especially at the corner of Worcester Street and Corporation Street and outside the Grand Hotel the players came in for great cheering.'

At the reception Foster responded with the captain's reply:

> On rising Mr Foster met with a hearty greeting. He said he felt that day was the greatest of his life and he thanked all present for the kind reception given the team. He felt it a great honour to be captain of a championship team like that and he could safely say they had done all that could have been wished of them. They had been triers and sportsmen all through. They had done everything they possibly could to help him, and he thanked them most sincerely. If there was a member of the team who deserved special mention, that was Frank Field. He was sure they would agree his bowling had been a feature of the season and had contributed greatly to the success achieved. William Quaife, as they all knew was one of the greatest men Warwickshire ever had. During the season when the team was in a hole, who pulled them out? Quaife. No mistake, he had been the mainstay of the team throughout the season. He had been magnificent – not only his batting and his bowling, but his fielding had been splendid. Having expressed regret at the absence of Kinneir, Mr Foster referred to the approaching visit to Australia and wished both Kinneir and Smith every success. Referring to Charlesworth, the speaker said he regarded him as the finest bat in England, bar none. If the team was in a hole, he always went in with smiling face, and usually came out with a more smiling face. If it had not been for his performances in the last few matches they would not be in the position they occupied today. Special mention should be made of Frank and George Stephens. These two he looked upon as two of the finest amateurs Warwickshire cricket had ever known. Concluding, Mr. Foster said he was glad to do what he had for the club.

Foster's citing Field for special mention acknowledged not only his outstanding bowling – he obtained a career-best 122 championship wickets at 19.48 – but his bravery. Throughout the season he suffered great pain from an old elbow injury, an injury incidentally which prevented his straightening his right arm and caused some people to accuse him of

---

40 The correspondent was probably Unite Jones, a large man who once got stuck in an Edgbaston telephone booth.

throwing. Plus ça change. In fact Field found it impossible to throw overarm at all.

Foster himself, in unpublished writings, described what happened in one 1911 match:

> Field was bowling poorly and in obvious agony. 'What's the matter with him?' I asked 'Tiger' Smith. 'Take him off,' he replied. 'Want a rest?' I asked Field at the end of an over. 'Don't be a fool, skipper. If you take me off there will be no-one to bowl,' he replied. 'Put your sweater on and clear off the field,' I replied. To my surprise he did leave the field and the twelfth man stayed on until luncheon.

> After my usual rub-down I went round to see Frank during lunchtime, but couldn't find him in the dressing rooms and asked where he was. 'Tiger' replied, 'Having a bath somewhere I think.' He wasn't. My hero was holding his elbow under a cold-water tap trying to ease the pain a terrible blow had caused years before.

Elsewhere, in 1933, when asked the reasons for Warwicks' success, Foster wrote:

> In the words of a contemporary Yorkshire professional who expressed his pleasure playing again them 'Warwickshire are a happy family'.

> Now isn't that lovely. If you don't think so you don't know the meaning of sportsmanship. From 1911 until war broke out Warwickshire were the happiest family of cricketers the world will ever see. We played the game as it should be played; our motto was 'Get on or get out'.

> I can honestly say that both on the field and off the Warwickshire team were as true to each other as a son should be to his father. We were more than great pals, we were 'great scouts' to each other. We blended together in a truly remarkable way, and that, to my mind, was the secret of our phenomenal rise. Perhaps the following may cause the reader to sit up and take notice:

> a) hot summer with dry, fast wickets prepared by one of the best groundsmen in England, John Bates, whose son has made many a hundred for Warwickshire;

> b) the wicket-keeping of 'Tiger' Smith;

> c) the magnificent bowling of Frank Field;

> d) the advice of Warwickshire's secretary, R.V.Ryder;

> e) the friendliness of those thousands of spectators keen enough to patronise Warwickshire;

> f) fate, in the shape of a new cricket ball, and a lady's name I cannot mention because the lady is the main cause of Warwickshire beating Northamptonshire for their thirteenth win of the season. Sorry friends, cannot spin out that yarn;

g) absurd changes of bowling;

h) Confidence, the keynote of all success. A batsman should walk to
the wicket with only one idea uppermost: 'My bat is going to
triumph over any bowler on this field.' Sadly I have seen many cases
of sheer funk displayed in the faces, even the speech of really
first-class batsmen prior to their walk to the wicket. No wonder
they have soon been back again, taking off their pads.'

Despite misgivings in some quarters, Warwicks' winning the title was
generally enthusiastically greeted. 'Pavilion Gossip' in the 2 September
issue of *Cricket* said:

The success of Warwickshire in securing the championship has been
marked by an enthusiasm which has been remarkable. From all parts of
the country, congratulations have poured in upon Mr Foster, and right
well have they been deserved, for the enthusiasm and ability the young
captain has displayed have been the means of increasing the
attractiveness and match-winning capacity of the side to an extent it
would be difficult to over-estimate. After their match with Surrey at
The Oval early in the season, Warwickshire seemed the county least
likely to carry off the chief honours of the year, and at the risk of being
told it is dangerous to use superlatives, we state that the whole history
of the game might be searched in vain for any more dramatic incident
than the recent advance of the side. It is a good thing for the game that
the championship should fall to the lot of a team which has never
before experienced such success and Mr Foster and his men are
thoroughly deserving of the many kind things which have recently been
said in their praise.

The writer is believed to be J.N.Pentelow, a well-known cricket journalist,
and he, at least seems aware of the part played by the 22-year-old genius,
Frank Foster. An alternative view is given in the following issue of the same
magazine, though the columnist, R.S.Holmes, stresses the ideas are not his:
'Is not Kent the stronger county, with 17 wins to Warwickshire's 13, each
having the same number of losses, 4?' Holmes then mentions those who
gravely inform everyone that 'by the previous two or more methods of
placing the counties Kent would occupy premier position.' 'Unconscious
humorists all,' averred the splendid Holmes. 'A team has to play under, and
if necessary adapt to, contemporary conditions, not those of the past.
Warwickshire did this admirably and so won the title.'

The fact is that the counties agreed to the new points system – five points
for a win, three for first-innings lead in a drawn game, one point for the
other side, the winners being the team with the highest percentage of the
points possible for them to obtain. Warwicks obtained 74 of a possible 100
points, having played 20 matches, therefore 74% while runners up Kent
played 26 matches but gained only 96 of a possible 130 points, therefore
73.84%. Looking at the overall statistics of the summer, Warwickshire's
success in jumping from fourteenth in the competition to first can be

largely attributed to the increased success of their bowling. In 1910 they had taken their wickets at 27.20 runs apiece, with only two sides having a higher figure. In 1911, wickets were secured at 22.83, and only four sides – one of them being Kent – had a lower figure.

It was unfortunate that Warwicks were obliged to play the annual Champion County *v* England at The Oval. They had run out of steam and were probably unprepared mentally for a match in which the champions almost always did badly.

Though lacking Kinneir, with lumbago, the champions' batting, with the Stephens twins, and Parsons at No.8, looked strong enough. The bowling was a worry though; Quaife, Santall and Charlesworth, none in the first flush of youth, had shown signs of tiredness. There was still the lion-hearted Field of course, seemingly immune to the strains placed on his near 37-year-old body, but even he was human, as his elbow problems had shown. Foster, who had had a few days rest with relations in Pontefract, won the toss but the innings was a disaster, right from when Lancashire's Dean removed Tiger Smith for a 'duck'. Foster appeared listless while making an unhappy 15 and, in two and a quarter hours, Warwicks were dismissed for 129. Dean took four wickets but the most impressive bowler was 20-year-old leg spinner, J.W.Hearne. His five wickets, Foster included, proved the value of a young spinner if given the opportunity. England went easily to 162 for one at the close, Hobbs and Mead going well. What followed was agonising; England batted well into the third day (of four) before declaring at 631 for five. Hobbs fell for 97, caught behind off Foster, but Philip Mead and C.B.Fry both scored centuries[41] and P.F.Warner a magnificent 244, a career best, which seemed to augur well for England's forthcoming Ashes series, when he would be skipper.

Contemporary reports say the fielding never flagged, but there were some horrendous bowling figures. Poor, worn-out Frank Field conceded 181 in 48 overs without even the consolation of one wicket and in fact no Warwicks bowler has ever conceded so many runs without reward. Foster's 38 overs cost 155 runs, but he did have the wicket of Hobbs. One does wonder about Foster, taking advantage of Field in such a manner. Perhaps he would have been excused had he lost his appetite for cricket yet he gave lion-hearted and effective service until his fortieth year, only war putting a break on his activities.

A day and a half left and 502 needed to force England to bat again: then another disastrous start, with opener Parsons run out at 13 going for a risky run! Rain gave brief hope of a draw, but it only freshened The Oval wicket, and before lunch on the fourth day Warwicks had lost by an innings and 365 runs, still their heaviest defeat. What an anti-climax.

At dinner at the Grand Hotel on Thursday, 21 September, Foster was presented with a token of appreciation for his leadership and Lilley

---

41   Fry's fourth century in succession; only he had done better, with six in 1901.

received a gift to mark the closure of his 24-year career. The local press described the celebrations:

> The Warwickshire eleven were entertained at dinner in recognition of their success in winning the championship. The Earl of Warwick presided and among those who assembled to honour the victorious team were Viscount Cobham, the Mayors of Warwick, Coventry and Sutton Coldfield and Messrs G.L.Jessop, G.A.T.Vials, J.Shields, M.C.Bird, L.C.Docker, H.W.Bainbridge, F.S.Goodwin, W.Ansell, G.Howard Cartland, H.O.Whitby, J.F.Byrne, J.A.H.Catton, C.Stewart Caine, S.H. Pardon, G.J.Groves, J.N.Pentelow, and F.S.Ashley-Cooper. Many unable to be present sent messages of congratulation. The toast 'The Club' was proposed by Lord Cobham, who referred to the connection and rivalry between Warwickshire and Worcestershire. 'What I like to see,' said his Lordship, 'is a good, dense ring of partisans. I like to see the better side win, when it is my own side.' (Laughter) After remarking it is important the County Championship continue, he congratulated Warwickshire on the splendid side they had put into the field. The team had been electrified by Mr Foster, who always tried to bowl the best ball he could and did not allow 'half-wide' off balls to go unpunished. Finally Lord Cobham paid tribute to Mr Cartland's labours on behalf of the club.
>
> Mr Cartland, on replying to the toast, asked why Warwickshire had not been champions before. The success of the side had provoked criticism; but Warwickshire did not make the rules, they agreed to them. However they had made a suggestion that every county should play all the others at least once in a season.
>
> G.L.Jessop was entrusted with the toast of the Warwickshire cricket eleven. He said even had they not won the championship they would still have deservedly stood out as team of the season. (Applause) They played the game in a live and truly sporting spirit. Mr Frank Foster, the outstanding figure, proved himself a captain of ready resource and with a useful knowledge of the numismatic bodies in their correct relation to gravity and a great all-round cricketer. Everyone hoped rumour was false and that Mr Foster would continue to lead the county for many years to come. (Applause). After referring to the fine performances of several players he finally congratulated Warwickshire on rising from the posterior position in 1910 to the 'Fosterior' position they now enjoyed.

Foster, it was reported was accorded 'a remarkable reception' on rising to respond and said it would be idle to pretend he was not delighted that the champion county was Warwicks. He spoke appreciatively of the way his team had supported him; how Field had taken a record number of wickets – and made nearly as many runs? (Laughter); how Kinneir had made the highest-ever score; how Quaife had stopped the rot on many occasions, and so on.

In response to popular clamour, Lilley, Quaife and Field all made short speeches before the Earl of Warwick gave all the amateurs and Lilley gold cigarette cases, Lilley a gold watch-chain too, and Foster a fitted dressing case. The event was concluded with various further toasts. Guests, players and captain then wended their way to cab, train and bus. Perhaps things were never the same again, but one last reference to 1911. Frank Foster personally enjoyed the most marvellous season ever for a Warwicks allrounder. His figures – never since even approached – were in his eighteen championship matches: 1,383 runs at 44.61, with a highest score of 200, ten catches and 116 wickets at 19.15. In all Warwicks first-class matches, twenty of them, he scored 1,459 runs at 42.47 and took 124 wickets at 19.68. He played three other first-class matches, giving him grand totals of 1,614 runs in forty innings at 42.47; 12 catches; and 141 wickets at 20.31, off 952.5 six-ball overs.

These are the bare bones. Figures do not convey the way he played; that for all scores over 50 he averaged more than a run a minute, that he captained a team regarded as 'no hopers' to the title, as the youngest-ever captain to take the Championship. Then there was the first 1,000 runs/100 wickets 'double' for Warwicks in a championship season. He repeated it in 1914. Since then only Tom Cartwright, in 1962, emulated the feat for Warwickshire with, in 27 championship matches, 1,082 runs and 101 wickets.

Foster remained an all-round force until the war of course, yet one feels he reached his peak in 1911. The 'Rosebud' syndrome maybe?

The cover of the menu at the dinner celebrating Warwickshire's championship success of 1911.
Foster is in the centre.
Clockwise from the top the other players are E.F.Field, W.G.Quaife, S.P.Kinneir, G.W.Stephens, C.Charlesworth, J.H.Parsons, C.F.R.Cowan, E.J.Smith, A.B.Crawford, C.S.Baker, W.C.Hands, F.G.Stephens, S.Santall and A.F.A.Lilley.

In good company.
Birmingham's finest included figures from politics, science, entertainment and sport.

Chapter Six

Under the Southern Cross

It had been a wearing, even manic season but six days after the Grand Hotel dinner Foster, Kinneir and Smith left for Australia. One imagines their desire for calm seas and a restful voyage.

It is doubtful whether any of the Warwicks trio featured in the selectors' plans at the season's start. As the season unfolded – as it became apparent that Warwicks could take a place among the giants – speculation became rife. On 30 June the selectors decided to invite Foster, and C.B.Fry was named prospective captain. Other amateurs invited were P.F.Warner and Lancashire's R.H.Spooner, while professionals Hobbs, Rhodes, Barnes and Strudwick were also asked. Then, at Fry's suggestion, James Iremonger, Nottinghamshire's experienced allrounder (who was never to play a Test) and the Essex pace bowler C.P.Buckenham were named. In July other places were confirmed; Jack Hearne, 20-years-old Middlesex allrounder was invited, as were Foster's wicket-keeper Tiger Smith and opener Sep Kinneir. Neither had yet played Test cricket. Surrey's Tom Pawley was named manager, but he accepted the position only when assured that the £170 he would lose as absent Surrey secretary would be matched by MCC.[42] Fry, citing his duties at *T.S.Mercury* – didn't his wife run the place? – and Spooner then dropped out and the captaincy reverted to P.F.Warner, who immediately demanded that his wife accompany him and have her fare and expenses paid by MCC. Thankfully the demand was refused. With J.W.H.T.Douglas, the Essex skipper, strengthening the amateur contingent and Phil Mead, George Gunn, Joe Vine and Bill Hitch (*vice* Buckenham) added to the professionals' brigade – the last two at the suggestion of the amateurs – the party was complete.

The send-off from Fenchurch Street Station on 29 September was enthusiastic, the platform so packed with well-wishers the players took thirty minutes to reach their carriages. However, the feeling of several self-styled 'experts' was that the team was not sufficiently strong. The party embarked from Tilbury on the Orient liner *R.M.S.Orvieto*. The weather was pretty good until they approached Naples when players who had played shipboard games and eaten heartily were suddenly unable to leave their cabins due to 'mal de mer'. Further disappointment came when at Naples they were confined to the ship due to cholera in the city. They then wended their way to Taranto; again no-one was allowed ashore but

---

42 Looked at through twenty-first-century eyes it seems incredible he even had to ask.

some locals rowed out to the ship and regaled the 'prisoners' with a rendering of 'God save the King'. It was barely recognisable and the players responded by throwing coins down the ends of the accompanying 'orchestra's' instruments. At Port Said, the party was allowed ashore for three hours; the heat was intense and Warner in particular felt drained.

HONOURS.

The Warwickshire Bear :—What d'yer think now, Mr. Foster? They want yer to fetch them "ashes!"

England expects.
Foster was sent to win The Ashes.

The party arrived at Colombo on 21 October and pith helmets were supplied for protection. Among the welcoming group were well-known cricketers Frank Crawford of Leicestershire and Somerset's W.T.Greswell, both there planting tea. Greswell in particular found little satisfaction, suffered depression and on his return to England became increasingly eccentric. MCC won a light-hearted one-day match by 213 to 59; Foster did his bit with a merry 36 and three cheap wickets. The party set sail for Fremantle, docking there on 31 October.

Foster seems to have enjoyed the voyage with Douglas acting as his protector. Ship's games, eating, drinking, dancing and flirting; all were to Foster's liking. He came close to disaster at the Colombo Club. After a drinking session and a meal, '... I signed so many chits I was under the table, or near enough.' Douglas was forced to cajole him into a waiting rickshaw so they would catch the boat and, because they were not making sufficient speed, Foster leaped out, got between the shafts and pulled Douglas to the waiting ship. He was immediately ordered to bed by Warner 'like a naughty child'.

The tour began with South Australia at Adelaide and despite the presence of Test man Clem Hill and eccentric ex-Surrey allrounder Jack Crawford, MCC won by an innings. Foster was one of three centurions with the highest debut score for a Test tour in Australia. His 158 in 162 minutes was magnificent. He dominated a stand of 157 with Warner and scored all but ten of a 60 partnership with Douglas. Foster and Barnes then scythed through the first innings, Foster four for 58, and he took another, for 24 in the second innings. A tremendous start but sadly Warner, unwell on the voyage, was taken ill following the game and did not play again on tour, Douglas taking over the captaincy.

An arduous train journey and the first Victoria game; MCC won a close contest by 49 runs and another Foster century created most appreciation. His 101 out of 133 with 13 fours came in only 134 minutes. Foster added 107 with Douglas, who scored 33 unbeaten out of 179 while he was in, prompting an exasperated crowd to award the soubriquet 'Johnny Won't Hit Today'. Tiger Smith and Kinneir made their tour debuts and acquitted themselves well though the latter – forty years old and ponderous in the field – may have realised his may be a marginal role but there would have been no worries about his value as a team man.

After another terrible train journey, lasting 17 and a half hours in intense heat and with only basic facilities, the party arrived in Sydney to an enthusiastic welcome and a civic reception. Warner, journeying by ship, arrived late, but in time for the start of the New South Wales game. Rain saw a disappointing draw but Foster bowled well, his three wickets including Trumper and Warren Bardsley, both caught behind by Strudwick. About this game, Strudwick wrote in 1959: 'I gave Foster the signal to bowl one outside leg stump for me to try and stump Duff, who I thought might move his right foot. Instead Foster sent the ball very wide of off stump and four byes resulted. The second time I signalled I made sure he saw what I meant. This time he bowled the ball straight to Frank Woolley at first slip. Then I realised he did not intend to give me the chance which he might have allowed had "Tiger" Smith, his own county wicket-keeper been behind the stumps.'[43]

---

43 Comment of this nature, from a wicket-keeper whose incompetence let England down on this tour, is disgraceful. In fact Duff did not play in this match: indeed he had last played first-class cricket in December 1907. Since this was the issue of *Wisden* which included Foster's obituary, it puts the editing and Strudwick's 'ghost' in a poor light. Tiger Smith informed this writer years later that, on this tour, Strudwick simply could not 'handle' either Barnes or Foster.

Moving to Brisbane, for the last State game before the first Test, MCC met an undistinguished Queensland side whose most charismatic member was the talented but undisciplined ex-Surrey player Alan Marshal. In Queensland's second innings Foster scythed through the first four batsmen, finishing with six wickets, Barnes had four and MCC ran out easy winners, after Foster hit a merry 33 not out, including an all-run six with Mead.

There followed a two-day game at Toowoomba. Following an enthusiastic welcome at the Town Hall, alcohol flowed freely, and the gathering degenerated into a hilarious shambles. In a nice little holiday, Rhodes took his only wickets of the tour and Foster had four cheap victims. Outstanding for Toowoomba was a 15-year-old, Eric Knowles. Sadly, forecasts of a bright future after a century on Sheffield Shield debut were not realised, mainly due to lack of opportunity.

The party returned to Brisbane to take on an 'Australian XI', a mixed bag under the captaincy of Trumper and including the ubiquitous Jack Crawford.[44] The 'Gabba' doubled as a trotting track and, in his tour book, Jack Hobbs mentioned that though not a betting man he made 18 pence as unofficial bookie for the other players. One wonders at the feelings of the 'proper' bookmakers; more importantly had Foster yet caught the gambling bug which served him so badly in later years? Later in the tour the party were Lord Duncan's guests at a Melbourne race meeting and Foster 'ran through the card'. Leslie Duckworth remarked in his *Story of Warwickshire Cricket* the advice proffered by Foster to keep within your limits when betting was not advice he himself followed in later years.

MCC made a disastrous start, losing four wickets, including Foster's, to the pace of John McLaren but determined batting by Kinneir helped MCC to 247. Kinneir's innings, watched close-up by Douglas, probably won him his first and only Test call aged 40, just days later. MCC held out for a three-day draw after some indifferent play from Foster, and contentious umpiring. Now on to Sydney and something more important: the First Test.

This commenced on 15 December, and selection options were limited by Warner's illness and injury to Hitch. Joe Vine, as twelfth man, Iremonger, and Tiger Smith also sat the match out. Skipper Douglas, Foster, Hearne, Kinneir and Mead made their Test debuts and to worshippers of experience England would have been on a loser from the start. So it turned out.

Things started badly; Clem Hill elected to bat and Douglas had the effrontery to take the new ball with Foster, despite having, in Barnes, the best new ball bowler in the world. Douglas had travelled to Sydney by sea

---

44   Crawford, a Surrey vicar's son and a great player in his youth, was sacked by Surrey for indiscipline and emigrated to South Australia to be player-coach and teach at St Peter's College, Adelaide. Personal indolence and character faults saw things again go awry and it must have been a relief to the cricket authorities when he did a 'flit' to New Zealand, albeit leaving behind a mountain of debt and a wife and child. Small wonder the SACA committee resolved to take more care over future imports.

with Warner and had arrived only an hour before toss-up. Had he spent time with his players he would surely have gauged their feelings and realised Barnes was his new-ball 'ace'. On taking the field England seemed to have little forward planning, nor did they know what fielding positions to take. Little wonder Australia reached 447 in good time. Trumper obtained his final Test century; not one of his best, but the kidney complaint, soon to prove fatal, was perhaps already affecting him. Best knock came from Test debutant Roy Minnett. He scored 90 in 111 minutes and when finally caught by Foster off Barnes, the catcher expressed regret at robbing him of a debut century. Neither Foster nor Barnes bowled well, and the former took his only two wickets at the end, when he at last had Barnes as his partner. Douglas had shown himself an action skipper, but woefully lacking in psychology.

In reply England had lost five for 142 when the youngest members of the side, Hearne and Foster, came together to add 89 in 62 minutes. Foster scored 56 from 76 balls, with nine fours – electrifying cricket on his Test debut – and he and the more sedate Hearne were largely instrumental in enabling England to reach 318. Australia's second innings saw superb bowling from Foster, dismissing Bardsley, Hill and Armstrong and later returning to deal with Hordern and Carter, ending with five for 92 in 31.3 overs. Despite Foster's effort, England started their second innings needing 438, and the task became even less realistic with the early demise of Hobbs. With time immaterial they did manage to grind on until the sixth morning but after Foster fell to Hordern's leg-spin (for the second time) for 21, they gently subsided to a 146-run defeat. Apart from Douglas' indifferent captaincy, the ineffectiveness of Barnes (four for 179 in the match) was disappointing, as also was the fact that their three most experienced batters Hobbs, Rhodes and Gunn failed to build on good starts. Strudwick had problems with Foster's leg-theory while Rhodes was now of no account as a bowler. But there was Foster whose fine half century, when badly needed, and match figures of seven for 197 marked a debut of which most cricketers would be proud.

Christmas was spent in Melbourne, Warner going to bed, but the rest enjoying as traditional a Christmas day as possible in a private hotel room.

The Second Test started at Melbourne on 30 December. Douglas, Foster, Hobbs and Rhodes met in Warner's hotel room and Warner immediately suggested to Douglas that Barnes, and not the captain, should open the bowling. Douglas initially disagreed, pleading that he bowled best with the new ball, but was finally persuaded. Thus a disgruntled captain, but the launch of a new ball pairing which was to play a pivotal role in regaining The Ashes.

Kinneir saw his Test career brought to a close; Rhodes moved up to partner Hobbs and fast bowler Bill Hitch came in, a logical step given the lack of an effective fourth bowler at Sydney. Behind the wicket Strudwick, suffering a slight back strain was replaced by Tiger Smith, experienced against Foster and a better bat. Australia won the toss on a lovely morning and no doubt they and the enthusiastic crowd looked forward to a big score against a toiling attack. Foster took first over, a maiden, but Barnes' first delivery hit Bardsley on the heel and rebounded onto the stumps. Kelleway, Hill and Armstrong then fell to Barnes in quick succession and the home side were 11 for four – in perfect conditions – all having fallen to Barnes for one run. Hobbs wrote that at this point Hitch remarked to him, 'Jack, we've won the match' as they crossed between overs, hands in pockets.

Foster then bowled Trumper, Barnes dismissed Minnett and at 38 for six, Barnes' figures were five for 6. Now feeling unwell he took no more wickets, and Australia reached 184. Barnes' final figures were five for 44, Foster had only one for 52 in 16 overs, but it must be stressed that conditions favoured the batsmen. Most people thought the last wicket had fallen at 144 when Bill Whitty was given out caught behind, but as the players approached the wicket gate it was noticed that Tiger Smith had remained in the middle in conversation with the umpire. Smith insisted he had not dismissed Whitty fairly so everyone returned to the middle and Whitty and Hordern added a further 40 runs. England then scored a disappointing 265 and owed much to J.W.Hearne, whose century was compiled, at age 20 years 324 days, the youngest for England in Australia. Second knock Australia again suffered an early collapse, four down for 38. Armstrong and Ransford then added 97 before the latter was taken by Smith off Foster. Armstrong went on to 90, but was never comfortable against Foster. He once almost swung himself off his feet trying to swish Foster to leg and after edging a four dangerously close to off stump Armstrong hit over Foster's yorker. The ball nicked Armstrong's pads on its way to his stumps and Foster appealed for lbw. Seeing the ball hit the stumps Foster apologised to umpire Bob Crockett for an unnecessary appeal and Crockett replied that when on ten Armstrong had edged Foster to Smith but nobody had appealed! Thus Armstrong's fine innings ought to have been nipped in the bud. Australia finally left England requiring 219 to score for victory. The bowling of Foster (38-9-91-6) and Barnes (32.1-7-96-3) had been paramount in putting England on track but again the support given was mixed. Foster sat out the next picnic match, at Geelong, before the serious business of the Third Test, at Adelaide.

Australia again won the toss and batted: on a superb strip Foster came of age as a Test bowler. Australia were skittled for 133 in 197 minutes and Foster, bowling as never before, swinging in the air, sometimes with a late straightening, and varying his pace, with evidence of a subtle slower ball, dismissed Kelleway (breaking a stump), Hordern, Hill, Minnett (whose wicket was also split when being bowled) and Armstrong for 36 runs in 26 overs. He also forced Ransford to retire at 17/2 after striking his thumb with a lifter. With three close leg-side fielders to his usual leg-stump attack he was devastating, as the ball-by-ball analysis shows:

> ..1..1/....../w...../..1.../....../.....11/....../...1../.1...../....../......24.1../...../...11../
> ...w.1/1...../..2...../...11w/w..w../4.1...

[Unfortunately it has not been possible to find an official scorebook but the above, up to the dismissal of Minnett was found by the master Australian researcher Charlie Wat in the *Adelaide Register*. Despite painstaking match reports it is not possible to work out the remainder of the analysis though this writer feels it *likely* that Foster conceded 4 and 1 to Matthews in the over after dismissing Minnett.]

Armstrong top scored with 33 before being bowled trying to dab Foster to leg but was lucky to avoid a 'duck' when Foster fell over trying to take a return catch. Barnes, with three for 71, was the other main bowler and they were well supported in the field, especially by Tiger Smith who caught a Bardsley outside edge off Barnes and later stumped Clem Hill brilliantly on the leg side off Foster. The demise of Hill especially emphasised the value of familiarity between bowler and keeper. Before play Foster said to Smith that he had noticed when playing a leg glide, Hill dragged his back foot in front of the crease so if he was bowling when Hill came in Tiger was to creep up to the stumps as Foster ran up for his first ball and station himself close in outside leg stump. First ball was perfect for a Hill leg glide; out he waltzed thinking Smith was standing back, missed the ball and was stumped by a foot. Foster, ever after regarded his bowling in this innings as the best of his career.

England then amassed 501 in eight and a half hours, with Hobbs' and Rhodes' first-wicket stand of 147 taking them past the Australian total on the second morning. Dropped at least five times, Hobbs went on to 187 in 334 minutes and he became the first Test batsman to exceed 300 runs without dismissal. Later in the innings Foster scored 71 in 134 minutes, a quality innings more restrained than usual that remained his best Test score. The end was disappointing, Armstrong bowling him with a half volley and Foster later admitted he had lost concentration through beginning to think about the possibilities of a maiden Test century. He never had a better chance. Some late amusement was caused by Tiger Smith's method of playing Hordern's spin. He repeatedly marched up the wicket as the ball was bowled, provoking Hordern to ask why he didn't just take it out of his hand. Smith was eventually caught by Vine, substituting for Trumper, who had a leg injury. Some debate was caused during England's innings about Hordern and Kelleway using resin on their fingers.

Australia fought back, but their second innings total of 476 must have disappointed. Several players batted well but it remained for many years the best Test score devoid of a century. Hill maintained his habit of getting out in the nineties, though the England players felt he had been stumped for a duck, Hill did not walk and umpire George Watson declined the appeal. It takes a brave umpire to give the local hero and captain a 'pair'. Best knock came from wicket-keeper Sammy Carter. Sent in as nightwatchman he scored 72, annoying the bowlers with a mixture of cuts and snicks. Perhaps they had forgotten Carter was from Halifax. Although bowling Bardsley with a fast leg break, Foster took only one wicket for 103 and seemed listless. Barnes was best bowler with five for 105.[45]   England reached the 109 they needed to win, losing only two wickets.

Foster's successes were beginning to be appreciated, especially in his native city. For a week after this Test match there was a great placard over the New Street Picture House which read 'Come and See Frank'. It was assumed passers-by would know to whom the placard referred.[46]

Apart from the cricket some excitement occurred on the Sunday between days two and three. Invited to dine with the Governor of South Australia, Sir Day Bosanquet, the players arrived when a bush fire was threatening the governor's residence, Marble Hill, and they helped quell the blaze before much damage was inflicted.

The next first-class match was across the Bass Strait, with Tasmania at Launceston, and Frank Foster was skipper. The youngest-ever captain of an English touring team was only 22 but the previous English season had been the hugely successful Warwicks captain, and as the only amateur in the side was the logical choice under the code of the time. Perhaps official thoughts were that here was a future Test captain. Sadly such hopes were to collapse dramatically.

Tasmania, omitting one of the best wicket-keepers in Australia, Norman Dodds, for sad, some may say disgraceful, non-cricketing reasons (alleged peccadilloes involving the wrong sort of sexual orientation) did well to reach 217, though Foster's non-use of either himself or Barnes detracted from the seriousness. Barnes opened the batting instead, contributing 35 towards MCC's 332 made in less than four hours, though things may have been different had Tasmania possessed a capable wicket-keeper. Tasmania then compiled a somewhat dour 165 against an attack again lacking its best bowlers and England went on to an eight-wicket win. The 19-year-old debutant Lyn Gill must have been particularly disappointed when stand-in keeper Llew Thomas dropped Woolley off his second ball in first-class cricket: 'it is such stuff as dreams are made on.' Good start as skipper, with MCC winning, but Foster had not taken his own performances very seriously.

MCC then went on to Hobart, Foster again leading. This time Barnes opened the bowling and his first ball saw W.K.Eltham caught by Foster. Tasmania struggled to 124 all out. MCC quickly lost Kinneir but then Woolley joined Rhodes and they added 206 in 100 minutes. Woolley was in fact down at No.8, with Mead No.3, but expressed his frustrations to Barnes who told him to get ready to bat and take the field as soon as the first wicket fell. Foster recounted what happened next:

---

45   In a big innings Rhodes was given only one over for six runs. Age 34 he had long been a spent force as a Test bowler; despite a very brief comeback late in life he was at his best before thirty, disproving the myth that Test slow bowlers improve with age, a wasteful theory that has never borne scrutiny.

46   This picture house had a cricket connexion of a sort. It was right next to the site of the Hen and Chickens hotel, where the first tour to Australia in 1863/64 was organised.

Barnes: Give young Frank a chance skipper, and put him in early.
Foster: What for? He can't bat.
Barnes: I'll tell you what I'll do. You've got Phil Mead down at No.3, so I'll go and lock him up somewhere.
Foster: What are you going to do with him?
Barnes: You leave it to me. There's a nice little room round the corner.
Foster: Hurry up then, because old Sep Kinneir won't last long. He's a Warwickshire boy.
Barnes: You're a Warwickshire nut! I wish you had been captain when I was tried for Warwickshire.
Foster: Shut up you silly old man. You can't bowl.

Barnes then got hold of Mead and locked him in a cloakroom. When Kinneir was dismissed for 26, Woolley grabbed his bat and hared out to the middle. Barnes had already told Foster of course, and the easy going skipper had good-humouredly concurred with the ruse but, no-one having told Woolley (or Mead), Woolley still assumed it was a secret between him and Barnes. This was a rarely seen example of Barnes' lighter side.

Following Rhodes' dismissal Woolley and Hearne added a further 264 in 100 minutes and Foster finally declared at 574 for four made in 270 minutes at more than a run a ball, with Woolley's 305 not out the highest-ever in Tasmania. The home side did much better second time around but still lost by an innings. Figures of three for 74 suggested Foster still did not take Tasmania seriously but he was a winning captain ... again.

Foster sat out the next game, with Victoria at Melbourne, and three days after this match the Fourth Test commenced on the same ground and England recovered The Ashes in brilliant style despite an enforced change – Vine for the injured Hitch – giving fewer bowling options. For once Douglas received the rub of the green, right from when he won the toss and inserted Australia on a grassy pitch. The home batters again let themselves down. Bardsley, all at sea against Foster, struggled for 20 minutes without scoring before he went out to drive, then decided to play to leg, finally did neither and had his stumps spread-eagled by Foster. Trumper struggled before being bowled by Foster and, after Barnes took wickets, Foster came back to get Ransford and Minnett caught by Rhodes; the latter's 56 was by far the best knock of the innings. Barnes wrapped things up; a total of 191 was far from adequate, as Hobbs and Rhodes demonstrated. They added 323 for the first wicket, at the time a Test first-wicket record and still the best stand for England in Australia.

Most of England's men scored runs, Foster going merrily to 50 in 86 balls before a most unlucky dismissal. Fancying his chance against Armstrong, he let fly at a tempting half volley, the ball flattened Hordern at silly mid-on and Foster, in his own words 'thought I had killed him'. In fact the ball lodged in Hordern's sweater and with Hordern still on the ground, Hill screamed 'Howzat!' and to general amusement a perplexed Foster departed after an innings described as 'the most attractive batting in the match'. England finally reached 589 in 190.5 overs, at the time their best Test score.

Needing 398 to avoid the innings defeat Australia batted spinelessly. At 12 Kelleway departed, caught behind off Barnes and then Bardsley confirmed his distaste for Foster, who now referred to him, cruelly, as 'rabbit warren'. They subsided gently to an innings defeat, only Sammy Carter showing any backbone. Douglas was this time the most effective bowler, but was finely supported by Foster, three for 38 and Barnes. Irresolute batting enabled England to triumph with a basically three-man attack. For the second Test in succession Foster had made an aggressive fifty in his only innings, as well as bowling valuably. Had a 'man-of-the-series' award been made, he would have been well in contention.

On to Sydney, and the return with New South Wales, newly crowned Sheffield Shield winners, and outside the Test matches it promised to be the game of the tour. A 17-hour train journey was not the ideal preparation, but any suspicions of tiredness were soon allayed. Trumper won the toss and a large Sydney crowd sat back in the sun, doubtless expecting a run-filled day.

Doubts would have crept in right from the second ball however. Bardsley had pushed Foster for a single but then H.L.Collins, intent on establishing himself as a Test prospect, found himself baffled and defeated by the swing and pace off the pitch of his first ball. A few balls later it was 7 for two. Bardsley, having scrambled two singles, saw a Foster lifter strike the shoulder of the bat. Strudwick muffed the catch but deflected the ball to Gunn at slip. Barnes now had Syd Gregory brilliantly taken low down at second slip, by Foster, of course. Douglas and Woolley then came on to get rid of Macartney and Trumper, after which Foster returned to run through the later order, finally finishing off the innings for 106 in 145 minutes. What a day for young Frank Foster. Seven for 36 in 19.3 overs against the cream of State cricket in fine batting conditions. In their reply MCC had much for which to thank Rhodes, his 119 the backbone of a not too satisfactory 315. Foster, on 10, gave a return catch to Hazlitt, whose medium-fast variations puzzled all, as his seven wickets testified. Inspired by a magnificent unbeaten 186 by 42-year-old Syd Gregory, New South Wales made a better fist of things second time around, managing a total of 403. Foster again bowled poor 'rabbit-warren' Bardsley cheaply, sealing his fate for the final Test. His two wickets cost 53 and the best bowling came from Jack Hobbs. Needing 195, MCC strolled to an eight wicket victory, Rhodes helping himself to a second century of the match. This win, against disappointing opposition, put England in a good frame of mind for the final Test at Sydney – a dead game admittedly, but one Douglas and his men were anxious to win.

England won the toss and relying more on attrition than inspiration reached 324 in 129 overs. Woolley's 133 was the best innings for England and, incidentally the first hundred by an English left-hander against Australia. Foster never got going and was stumped off Hazlitt for 15. In its turn the much vaunted Australian batting again failed to do itself justice. They succumbed to 176 all out, Barnes, with three wickets getting best figures. Foster, perhaps tired – after all he had been his side's busiest player – and maybe missing his 'rabbit', Bardsley, had to be satisfied with a single wicket but was unlucky when he hit Gregory's stumps low and hard, but the bails stayed put. He regularly hit the batsmen on pads and thighs however and was the brunt of catcalls from the crowd. Cries such as 'bowl at the wickets' were surely indicative of an ignorant crowd's frustrations. A damp and dismal third day saw England bat poorly against the spin of Hordern and the slow cobs of Armstrong. They still gained a lead of 362 but, with unlimited time at their disposal, Australia was thought to have some hope. There was a blank sixth day but on day seven Australia seemed in with a chance before three late wickets for Foster saw them finish 71 short.

England had deservedly won The Ashes and owed a lot to Barnes, with a record beating 34 wickets but Foster, who had his twenty-third birthday between the Third and Fourth Tests and whose 32 wickets equalled the previous record, remain the best for a debut series for England. Often he seemed more threatening than his illustrious partner and he had marginally the better average – 21.62 against 22.88. Even when not taking wickets his leg-theory and variations sowed confusion and Bardsley especially had great difficulty against him. Then there was his batting: he scored 226 runs at 32.28, with an average scoring rate of 53 runs per 100 balls. Only Woolley, 63, and Hobbs, 56, exceeded him and neither did any bowling to speak of. His was perhaps the most exciting young talent in world cricket, a view supported strongly by his performances in all first-class matches. His 62 wickets, average 20.19 actually placed him top of the Australian first-class averages for the season, and he also took most wickets. Add to this his 641 runs, average 35.61, making him seventh top-scorer in the first-class season. The contemporary praise for him was unfairly muted. Not just contemporary praise; Barker and Rosenwater's *England v Australia*, published 1969, makes few references to one who on figures was the leading bowler and best allrounder for either side.

Foster's qualities were not completely unrecognised. In *Cricket* magazine former Australian captain Harry Trott wrote praising his 'grit [and] delightful crispness' with the bat and reckoned him second only to Barnes as a bowler, though questioning whether his physique would stand up to prolonged hard work.

Then there was the 'verse' in a later issue by a Kent railwayman called Cunningham. Though too awful for reproducing here the Foster reference is of interest:

> Then Douglas he acted just like a brother
> With excellent help from a good Foster-mother.

Mr Cunningham was pronounced another 'Albert Craig', so bad was he, but even this was overpraise; the new 'McGonagall' maybe?

On tour generally Foster made himself popular. He was friendly with hotel and bar staff, who probably appreciated the way he liked sampling local brews while his dress-sense was also noticed. Turning up for a match in plus-fours prompted a London fashion guru to comment: 'See Foster's trousers and die.' A New South Wales 'poet' signing himself Augustus Bails wrote:

> The flannel pants of Foster cost
> A guinea clear per pair.
> Hearne's work out rather less. Hobbs lost
> A tenner once – a rare
> Experience
> With him, his sense
> Of caution being strong.
> And, *apropos*
> It riled him so
> He cursed both loud and long.

David Rayvern Allen could not find a place for that one in his book of cricket poems 92 years on: a wise decision.

Despite Foster's general popularity *Cricket* does detect a whinge emanating from Australia, describing him as a 'damn intentional smasher of batsmen's fingers and batterer of batsmen's thighs.' *Cricket* replies though:

> Everyone who knows the Warwickshire captain – as genial and manly and true a sportsman as ever trod green turf – will be indignant at the cowardly and libellous imputation. And they said Frank Foster was such a favourite in Australia! One did not marvel at that. There is a winning charm about this young cricket genius that most of us feel; but one does wonder whether he cares much about losing the esteem of people who cannot accept defeat gracefully, but in the dark hours must fling such charges about. Though to be sure it is not likely that many people in Australia believe them.

It has not been possible to discover where that particular whinge appeared; doubtless Foster treated it with appropriate contempt.

As for Foster's humour, he was greatly amused at the circumstances surrounding the team group taken in a Melbourne park – it appears in this book on page 65 – before the Second Test. The original line-up had George Gunn seated on the extreme left next to Rhodes, with Strudwick immediately behind him. Hearne and Hitch were sat on the ground just in front of Douglas and Foster. It was then found that the ground under Gunn's chair was very rough so he took it and sat next to Hobbs on the extreme right. This would have upset the balance of the picture so Strudwick was asked to move to behind Gunn's new position, next to Vine. Hearne and Hitch stayed on the ground but moved a place to their right. No one seemed to realise that this left Foster in the middle of the seated row, in the place usually reserved for the captain. Little wonder that in among the cardboard expressions and serious faces Foster seems to have an almost child-like, but certainly genuine smile. An omen? This was apparently asked of Warner when he saw the photograph and he replied Foster would one day captain England. Unfortunately a 40 mph collision with a lamp standard in 1915, right leg stiffly extended to save himself from being killed, ruined any hopes of that.

Under the eucalypts in a Melbourne Park.
The MCC team which toured Australia in 1911/12.
Standing (l to r): S.Kinneir, E.J.Smith (wk), F.E.Woolley, S.F.Barnes,
J.Iremonger, R.C.Campbell (scorer), J.Vine, H.Strudwick (wk).
Seated: W.Rhodes, J.W.H.T.Douglas, P.F.Warner (capt), F.R.Foster,
T.E.Pawley (manager), J.B.Hobbs, G.Gunn.
On the ground: J.W.Hearne, J.W.Hitch.

Finally we cannot leave the 1911/12 tour without mention of Foster's 'affair', not with the mysterious Margaret, with whom he struck up a shipboard liaison, but with six-year-old Betty, daughter of Pelham Warner. She quickly took to the easy-going Foster and followed him around throughout the tour. No-one could explain the soubriquet 'porcupine' which she gave Foster as he carried her teddy-bear collection around Australia. Foster said in *Cricket Memories*:

> We were great pals, Betty and I, and for some unknown reason she nicknamed me 'porcupine'.[47] We loved each other very dearly, and were always playing together at some game or other. Just before I went into bat in the Second Test, Betty called out to me from her seat in the stand, 'Stick your bristles out porcupine, and show these kangaroos what my porcupine can do'.

---

47   Foster later claimed it had been explained to him by somebody, but it was 'dead secret'.

Foster once reflected that he had only ever had proper loving relationships with children or animals. A sad statement from someone perhaps already on an unstoppable slide towards personal disaster.

Action Man?
Posed photographs of Foster in the style of the time.

Chapter Seven

Vicissitudes down to war

On the party's return home a banquet was organised by MCC at the Hotel Cecil, off the Strand. At the MCC annual general meeting at Lord's on 1 May 1912, Foster, as an amateur team member, accepted MCC membership. Not a lasting honour unfortunately; by 1918 he had disappeared from the members' list, never to return. Meanwhile Warwicks organised a dinner for Foster, Kinneir and Smith. A profit of £510 was earmarked for ground improvements and 300 new members were announced, due, it was claimed to the 1911 successes, but more likely because of one man, Frank Foster. Finally Middlesex were to be played in 1912 – at last! Ominously Foster stated this was to be his last season; he should not have toured Australia and that he would definitely retire. He was described as a 'retiring' type, but one feels this talk was that of a troubled soul.

The 1912 season started with Foster and Smith playing in a 'Test Trial' for which there seemed little point. Then it was back to the Championship and Warwicks began their title defence with three wins out of three; most satisfactory obviously, though Foster was having a quiet time. Then another Test Trial: Foster contributed to his side's innings win with a bright 43 and six wickets but the futility of the match was emphasised by the inclusion of the 40-year-old Kent leg spinner D.W.Carr. He had played with limited success against Australia in 1909 and now, three years older and more portly, here he was again. Carr's figures were none for 91 this time. In 1909 critics felt the selectors had taken leave of their senses over Carr, but now they seemed lost for words. From farce to sadness; Frank Field had been chosen for The Rest but failed to turn up for no announced reason. In fact the invitation never reached Field. It had been sent to Edgbaston while Field was taking advantage of a short break between matches, resting in the country. He never had another chance.

Warwicks then took on Worcestershire, who had lost all three early matches. With Foster bowling brilliantly to take 11 for 131, Worcestershire capitulated. Four wins out of four and top of the table; a repeat of 1911? Sadly, far from it: something now went wrong and things were never the same again.

There was however a break from the Championship with the Australian tourists, over here with South Africa for the first, and last, triangular tournament, coming to Edgbaston. Warwicks batted indifferently in both innings but so did the tourists and Foster's incisive leg-theory brought him first innings figures of seven for 94 in 34 overs. Australia hung on for the draw. Bardsley confirmed his reputation as Foster's 'rabbit' and Macartney announced that in order to try and protect himself against leg-theory he had cut a pad in half and strapped it around his right thigh inside his trousers.

The popular venue at Wantage Road, Northampton came next but on a poor wicket only Quaife had the defensive technique to thrive. Foster took four for 33 but rain curtailed the match. An unsatisfactory end to a run of eight consecutive championship victories – still a Warwicks record.

Foster and Smith now went to Lord's for the first South African Test. The weather was uncertain but the wicket fairly dry. South Africa batted and in 157 balls, all bowled by Foster and Barnes, were all out for 58. Foster five for 16, Barnes five for 25 and E.H.D.Sewell, he who had sneered at Warwicks in 1911, damned Foster with faint praise, saying that two of his wickets were taken with balls that could almost be described as 'half volleys'. Sewell also criticised Smith's 'rustic' wicket-keeping. Despite a late collapse England gained a lead of 279. South Africa did somewhat better second knock; Llewellyn playing well for 75 and Aubrey Faulkner defending obstinately for 15 in 75 minutes, but finally succumbed for 217. Llewellyn's dismissal was interesting. He nicked a leg catch to Smith off Foster and it was reported that Smith moved across to leg as Foster started his run up; whether a plot hatched by bowler or keeper or both was uncertain but the now boring Sewell expressed disapproval. Llewellyn should actually have gone earlier; he skied Barnes to Fry at short leg and, according to Tiger Smith in his autobiography, 'it was a dolly catch but he went round in a circle waiting for the ball and when it came down he was yards away having run himself dizzy. He was so embarrassed he pulled the peak of his cap to the back of his head and disappeared into the long field, a strange place for a captain to go.' Shortly afterwards he again put Llewellyn down; fortunately for Fry England still won.

Back to the Championship and the seemingly none too onerous task of dealing with Leicestershire, winless and second last in the table. Defeat for Warwicks was out of the question, yet they lost in two days. The bubble had burst. Leicestershire batted first and reached 196, Foster taking five for 71, albeit all tailenders, and Warwicks replied miserably with 85 in 42.5 overs. Leicestershire left off 142 ahead but following an all-night poker session Foster was devastating and with Field skittled Leicestershire for 90. Foster had one spell of 12 overs, taking four for 11, and finished with seven for 21 in 19.2 overs. With 202 needed for victory and plenty of time remaining, Parsons and Baker took them to within 22 of the required target with five wickets in hand; then calamity. The last pair came together with ten needed but, when still four runs short, local footballer Jim Windridge panicked and was thrown out by Albert Knight. A first championship defeat in just under a year, to a team that had lost six of its seven previous games. As for Foster – twelve for 92, yet on the losing side – what had gone wrong?

A couple of unconvincing draws, then it was back to Test cricket for Foster and Tiger. Australia at Lord's on slow wicket in damp conditions. Though preferring fast wickets Foster was reasonably economical, taking two for

*Cartoon of Foster by his playing colleague
Charles Baker.
Baker was later a cartoonist for national
newspapers and a lightning artist on the
music halls.*

42 in 36 overs before rain ruined the game. It must have been a shock to read Hamish Stuart in *Cricket* advocating Foster's omission: England often treat their heroes shabbily.

On his return to the county scene Foster saw an unsatisfactory draw against Yorkshire, rain saving his side from a heavy defeat and he then joined Smith for the second South African Test at Headingley. Foster did well in support but Barnes spearheaded England's victory. Before returning to Edgbaston Foster and Smith had a Gentleman *v* Players game at The Oval. Of most interest was the return, after a long absence on state business, of the great Ranjitsinhji: he scored 24 and 42. The match included a short break as a mark of respect for former Test fast bowler Tom Richardson, whose funeral it was at Richmond but cricket-wise the game lacked interest and colour. Foster dismissed only Hobbs and Mead and scored four runs.[48]

Next Warwicks opponents were top-of-the-table Northamptonshire, going for a first title on the back of cracking wins over Kent and Surrey, and now

---

48   An odd feature of this game that at least four participants suffered mental illness. Fry suffered recurrent problems; Greswell (he became known as 'Mr Wells from Assam' on his return to England) never recovered from the depression suffered while tea-planting; Bert Relf was eventually driven to take his own life; and then there was Foster.

playing the fading champions. And Warwicks won overwhelmingly, by 303 runs, at the time their biggest 'runs' win: for several years it was also Northamptonshire's biggest beating. One can come up with no feasible explanation for such a sudden and complete – and for Warwicks, temporary – turn-around in performance.

Warwicks batted first and were given an excellent start by Smith and Charlesworth but collapsed from 237 for five to 247 all out. Northamptonshire were smartly dismissed for only 53 towards the end of the first day. Foster, with five for 22 in 14 overs, and Field, five for 27 in 13.2 overs, bowled unchanged – wonderful restoration of their 1911 form. Foster did not invite Northamptonshire to follow on and led by Smith's 91, Warwicks pushed on, leaving Northamptonshire a day and a half to make 464. The visitors submitted so abjectly they only just prolonged proceedings into the third morning. Best bowlers this time were Quaife, five for 30, and medium pacer Collin Langley, with three for 33. Langley became better known for non-playing activities at Edgbaston. His personal book collection became the basis for the Collin Langley Library, from 1998 until 2004 a popular refuge for supporters during lunch, tea or weather breaks.

In another championship break the Gentlemen took on the Players at Lord's but Foster declined his invitation, feeling needful of a rest. Warwicks now went to Lord's; Middlesex were contesting the top places, though it helped that most of their games had been at headquarters. The match was marked by poor weather and play and Middlesex owed much to 'old' Jack Hearne, whose nine wickets overshadowed his distant relation 'young' Jack. The team underachieved but the skipper still won praise for the way he refused to slow the game down when time was running out, enabling Middlesex to win with just two minutes left. After the match Warner wrote to Foster:

> Dear Frank,
>
> Unfortunately I was not able to play in the match just finished but I have heard all about it. Middlesex are proud of Warwickshire. Will you kindly tell Mr Ryder that he may choose any date he likes next summer for the continuation of such a friendly game as Middlesex has just had with Warwickshire.
>
> Yours as ever,
> Plum

This had been the first meeting of the counties and Middlesex and Warwicks now travelled up to Edgbaston, possibly together, for the return. The metropolitans as ever proved they were only half the team when forced to play north of Watford.

Conditions favoured the bowlers and although Tarrant showed his all round worth, he was excelled by Foster. In the Middlesex first innings Foster had five for 58 in 34 overs of unrelenting leg-theory and he received support from a 20-year-old debutant George Byrne, a nephew of ex-skipper Fred Byrne, who was brought on late and finished off the innings by dismissing the last three batters in four balls. Sadly Byrne's self-discipline did not match his talent. There was an incident involving a large potted plant at a hotel at Hastings late in the season and he played no more. A fine stand of 122 between Baker and Foster, whose restrained 56, his first half-century since early May, was ended by an unlucky run out, enabled Warwicks to set a target of 240 in more than a day. Then Foster, dispensing with his short-leg fielders, bowling slower than usual and turning the ball considerably from leg caused an after-lunch collapse, sending Middlesex to defeat with six for 29 in 21.4 overs, the last four wickets for seven runs in 28 balls. Rarely had he bowled with so much thought. Strange it was that this unbelievably talented cricketer did not revert to slow spin more often.

Foster and Smith now travelled to Old Trafford for the second Australian Test – a waste of everyone's time, rain allowing a mere five hours play: the bad weather followed them, and the rest of Warwicks' players over the Pennines to Hull. On a diabolical wicket Hirst and Drake skittled Warwicks for 59. Foster, seven for 42, and Field, three for 40, then sent Yorkshire packing for 88 and Warwicks reached 64 for three second time around before the sorry business, played after, during and before rain was called off. Worcestershire now came to Edgbaston. The Pear County were not having a good season – they finished bottom – whereas Warwicks retained realistic ambitions of a high place. Foster gave Worcestershire first use of a slow wicket, a shrewd move with no obvious motive and Collin Langley, first change, ran riot with his medium pace. His eight for 29 was not only a career best but remains an innings best for either side at Edgbaston in the series. Worcestershire were dismissed for 126, Warwicks replied with 171, before rain again intervened to ruin the game. Then Gloucestershire and despite Warwicks posting a total of more than 300 for the first time in the season at their headquarters, rain was again the victor. Foster's single wicket, for 50 runs, was his hundredth of the season.

The county now enjoyed a break while Foster and Tiger travelled to The Oval for the third South African Test. London had been as badly hit as anywhere by the wet weather. South Africa chose first use of a damp and unreliable wicket. Barnes and Woolley, five wickets apiece, were lethal and South Africa were dismissed for 95. Foster, six overs for 15 runs, may have felt cheated. England's reply was better but they eventually slumped to 176 all out against Faulkner's leg spin. The wicket on day two was a minefield, Barnes found 'spots' for his leg and off breaks, only left-hander Dave Nourse (42) exceeded ten, and South Africa were all out 93, with Barnes taking eight for 29 in 16.4 overs. They had been whitewashed by England, finding the weather and Barnes, with 34 wickets in three Test matches, average 8.29, too much. Foster again had little opportunity but did take a return catch to dismiss Nourse.

The Edgbaston season finished with a visit from Surrey, another side with early title aspirations but now, like their hosts, sinking without trace.

Thanks to 93 from Kinneir who had been suffering a torrid time, Warwicks reached 220; Surrey's much-vaunted batsmen then had no answer to the leg-theory of Foster, six for 53 in 16.5 overs. Only the less-celebrated and allegedly slow-footed Edward Goatly, getting his head down and his body behind for an unbeaten 35, enabling them to reach 130. Further rain then curtailed what had been a damp, dark and miserable home season for the deposed champions.

Foster missed the next two washed-out Warwicks matches to appear at The Oval against Australia in the last Test of the ill-fated triangular series. On a typically dead wicket, England outplayed Australia who, set 310 for victory collapsed alarmingly against 'second-string' bowling of Dean and Woolley; 65 was all they could muster. Nothing went right, the nadir being reached when a Hobbs throw hit the stumps with Bardsley well in his ground. Hobbs appealed and umpire John Moss ruled the batsman out. England did not need that sort of thing – they were winning anyway. As for Hobbs – did he have a conscience?

This frustrating match was Foster's last Test though obviously he was unaware of this: 19 and three not out, two overs for five runs and one catch (or was it two?). He reckoned he caught Syd Gregory off Dean in the second innings, put the ball in his pocket and he and Woolley then ran to the boundary in pursuit of an imaginary ball. Tiger Smith shouted at Foster to stop fooling about and throw the ball up: skipper Fry, maybe lacking a sense of humour, was non-plussed. The umpire gave Gregory out and reports and scorecards awarded the catch to Douglas. Strange goings on. The under-praised hero of 1911/12 had now been hindered by unsympathetic captaincy. Against Australia he had been insultingly underused, taking a mere two wickets for 50 in 39 overs. Then again for most of the season he was manifestly stale and, according to Tiger Smith years later, he bowled too much leg-theory and couldn't be bothered to think about the game. Still only 23 and his Test career over.

Foster returned to his county for their final three matches. Good results would have seen them well-placed but they were in freefall. The first matches of their southern tour featured Sussex at Hastings and Hampshire at Bournemouth, both marked by depressing weather and even more depressing play by Warwicks, easily beaten both times. Foster swished around aimlessly and though taking eight wickets he bowled very mechanically.

Finally to The Oval. A few days without rain had made the pitch hard and fast and it was interesting that Foster's first day 54 in 80 minutes was the best innings of the match and, for him, probably the best of the season. Warwicks had the better of a fine first day, but then damp misery returned and they lost by six wickets. Apart from his excellent first knock Foster seemed to just go through the motions, 18 overs for 55 runs and no wickets.

Thus the welcome end to a season that had turned into a nightmare. Warwicks seemed in need of a break, their skipper was physically and mentally exhausted. *Wisden* commented that Warwicks were essentially a hard-wicket team. Only Santall, of the bowlers, preferred slow wickets and he was a veteran. Foster's comparative failure was put down to the slow wickets, but also the heavy workload so young a player had endured during the past three years. A valid point; not common knowledge then was the fact that though on the face of it easy-going and physically robust he was physiologically and psychologically fragile. A delicate and over-tuned piece of machinery liable to snap at any time. *Wisden* stated that he never seemed fresh but ended on the happier note that a statement that 1912 was to be his last season was incorrect: 'All being well he will captain the Warwickshire XI for some time to come.' Perhaps, in hindsight, his frequent 'retirements' were a symptom of an underlying depression.

His 115 wickets at 17.40 seemed not too bad, and in fact he finished 24th in the first-class averages among bowlers with 20 or more wickets, as against 26th in 1911. On raw figures then he seemed to have done at least as well, yet did not seem to be so doing, and certainly he overdid the leg-theory and showed less variety. His batting, 727 runs at 18.81, definitely declined. The damp, slow wickets did not suit him; only when showing untypical restraint did he score runs. Rest was his hope of cricketing salvation.

Winter was spent at Wilkinson and Riddell and in the February issue of *Cricket* is the following announcement: 'After all Frank Foster is not giving up big cricket, and he will lead his county's team again this season. The importance of this fact can hardly be overestimated. There is no greater asset to a team than a skipper of the lifting type, a man who has confidence in his men and in himself – and such is Foster.' It went on: 'Neither Warwickshire nor England can afford to do without him for years to come yet, though whether his services will very long be available remains to be seen.'

Foster and Warwicks were also mentioned in an anonymous article titled 'The County Championship' in a later issue of *Cricket* magazine on 3 May. This complained that, by wishing to make county cricket more spectator-friendly, the authorities were in danger of pandering to the ignorant masses with no proper knowledge of the game. It commented: 'As an instance, one may cite the Birmingham crowd. Until Warwickshire began to do well in 1911 they had comparatively poor gates, but now large crowds assemble at nearly every match. Mainly because of Frank Foster, because of the glamour of his personality, to see him 'it 'em 'ard and 'i and horften – not to watch the game at all its varying aspects.'[49]

---

49   Apart from the anti-Warwicks and Birmingham stance – there was surely the same seething mass of ignorance on the popular side at The Oval, and other grounds – the writer seems to get his dialects mixed up. 'Horften' sounds lower-class 'Sarf London' or, without the 'h' Shropshire or the Welsh borders in general. The Brummie was likely to have used the older English 'offen'. Still, it proved that Warwicks and Foster had made a mark. Jealousy was in the air.

The 1913 season presented a possible difficulty even before it started. Having been appointed coach, Santall was not expected to play much but his semi-retirement led to a strengthening of the team, since his replacement was newly qualified Percy Jeeves who confirmed the wisdom of R.V.Ryder in persuading him to come to Edgbaston.

The opening game was with local rivals Worcestershire, played under the grey ruins of Dudley Castle, in even greyer weather. Actually Worcestershire seemed to be having the better of the exchanges until skipper H.K.Foster decided that his own half-century was more important that giving his side a realistic victory chance. When Harry Foster finally declared after his own dismissal for 58 only two hours remained to dismiss Warwicks, who themselves needed an unlikely 260 to win. Smith's aggressive 66 led a token victory effort before the game petered out to the inevitable draw, with Frank Foster not even bothering to bat. Small wonder he had little respect for the Rev Foster's boys.

First Edgbaston visitors were Leicestershire and a Quaife century and lethal bowling by Jeeves led to an easy win. Unfortunately the early form was not repeated against Derbyshire, despite five first-innings wickets for Foster. Derbyshire needed 261 on the last day and good batting by the amateurs Leonard Oliver and John Chapman, as ever a thorn in the Bears' paw, saw them home, with Foster strangely subdued, his 18 overs costing 58 runs.

Foster had so far scored only 33 runs in five innings and his 11 wickets had come from mainly unimpressive bowling, but any fears about his form and commitment were allayed when they visited Southampton to take on Hampshire. Foster won the toss but in no time four wickets were down; Foster then joined Quaife and they added 99 with Foster's share a quick 66. A total of 260 looked somewhat short when Hampshire reached 242 for five but a late collapse ensued, Foster took the last five wickets and Warwicks' position was strengthened when Foster promoted himself to No.3. In his best innings since 1911, he hit 16 fours as he pulled and scythed his way to 111 in less than two hours, dominating a fourth wicket stand of 111 with Baker. Hampshire's last-day target of 331 was always likely to be difficult but Phil Mead laid about him, scoring 170 in 190 minutes, his last 108 out of 124 but on his dismissal, Hampshire's challenge faded and Warwicks triumphed by 64 runs. Foster collected three more wickets to make it a hundred runs and eight wickets in a match for the fourth time. A glimpse of his glory days and the victory, gained with enterprise and adventure proved the value of Foster 'on song'. Unfortunately this form was not carried on to The Oval where Surrey should have been beaten had Warwicks scored more quickly and not allowed them to play for a draw. Foster had none for 55 in 17 overs in the first innings and feeling 'off colour' did not bowl at all on the final afternoon. E.H.D.Sewell remarked: 'Foster is bowling a different style from that which secured him so many wickets on the leg side, and seems to have shed for the time being much of that nip from the pitch which was his chief asset against batsmen who can bat.'

Northamptonshire now visited Edgbaston; Foster batted listlessly and after being too unwell to bowl in the first innings took only one for 52 second time. It was no surprise that he now went off to Prestatyn for a 'holiday' and missed the next two matches. Thankfully he returned for Middlesex at Lord's and it was stated that the cause of his recent problems had nothing to do with cricket; he had reportedly been 'larking about' at home with brother Arthur and hurt his side after a heavy contact with the corner of a sideboard.

Foster had ample opportunity to test out his fitness; on an excellent surface Middlesex reached 483, with centuries from Tarrant and Warner. Foster gave himself 39.5 overs for figures of four for 124, but though dismissing Warner, his other victims were the Hon Rupert Anson, N.E.Haig and G.G.Napier, an abundance of aristocratic connexions but none in the batting front rank. Warwicks' reply was eccentric; with no hope of a win they went on all out attack. Smith hit 33 out of 43 in 20 minutes, Charlesworth 60 in 80 minutes. Quaife restored sanity with 50 in more than two hours but six were down for 191 when Foster and Percy Jeeves came together and added 82 in 65 minutes, Foster, after beginning shakily scoring 70. Warwicks fell just one run short of saving the follow-on and suffered a disastrous second-innings debacle. Nought for one overnight they underwent an unbelievable collapse to 33 for nine. Then, and then only did Foster come in. He had only just reached the ground, not having expected to be needed so soon. Under the weather (again) after a heavy night he had taken Willie Hands to the Turkish Baths early in the morning. They then treated themselves to a shave, haircut and shampoo, and had a game of snooker before deciding to get a cab to Lord's.

Let Foster take up the story in his own words:

> We rolled up to Lord's and looked at the scoreboard. 'Good God,' shouted Hands and he ran like a stag up the long entrance to the dressing rooms. I thought the man had gone mad, but when I took a closer look I discovered that there were eight Warwickshire men out. Hands just managed to change at the fall of the eighth wicket, the Middlesex XI captained by Plum Warner waiting a few minutes for Hands. I had to bustle myself for once and just managed to be ready in time to go in last. Hands was still batting, I went in at 1 o'clock, Lunch was 1.30. As I passed Hands at the wicket I said: 'Stick it in and let me have the bowling as much as possible. We'll try and keep these beggars in the field all afternoon.' Hands winked and nodded. At 1.30 we were still together. Plum Warner said to me 'Shall we go on for a few more minutes Frank?' I replied 'Yes' and, damn me, if Hands didn't then get out. He had made three out of 30 between us; I had made the other 27.

Foster went on: 'The best joke was this. After we had lunched, packed our bags and returned to our hotel, I ran smack into my father as we were crossing Trafalgar Square. He said: "Where have you been?" "Why?" I replied. "Haven't you seen the newspaper placards?" I said "No". "Well," he said, all the placards had got it in big type, "Where's Frank?"'

This represented a most unsatisfactory state of affairs. A humiliating defeat with 'old' Jack Hearne having figures of five for 12 in 14 overs on the third morning and despite his late heroics with the bat, the skipper let himself and the side down by his arriving so late. Foster's *laissez–faire* style of leadership works well when the side is successful but can be disastrous at other times, as was shown here. There was no direction from the skipper, no inspiration, no advice, since he wasn't there. Worst of all he seemed to find humour in the situation.

If the Lord's game was a humiliation, what of the following match with Kent at Tonbridge? *Cricket* magazine explained away Warwicks' all out 16 in the second innings as 'Just one of those accidents which will happen now and again. A queer pitch, bowlers whom it exactly suits, bad batting by some men, bad luck for most and you get a score which does not reach a score. It looks worse when, as happened at Tonbridge, the other side goes in again and makes runs with seeming ease; but a bad pitch at 1 o'clock may be a quite decent one at three. And Foster had neither a Blythe nor a Woolley to call upon.' Did Warwicks' supporters treat the debacle with such serenity one wonders? It has remained the county's lowest first-class score and the lowest in any game involving Kent.

In fairness Warwicks played their first match in Kent in the twentieth century with a weakened side. Jack-of-all-trades Charles Baker deputised for the injured Smith. Kinneir, Field, Langley and the Stephens twins were unable to turn out. For two days they held their own. At the end of a rain interrupted second day Kent were 104 for five in reply to 262 and on the third morning excellent bowling by Foster – six for 62 in 29 overs, five of the last six wickets for 13 – and Jeeves dismissed the home side for 132. Warwicks commenced their second innings around midday with a lead of 132. Forty-five minutes and 10.2 overs later they were all out 16. The pitch was reported to be very bad: Blythe and Woolley, who both had figures of five for 8, found conditions entirely suited to their left-arm spin. But the fact was that no-one tried to block things out, as Quaife and Baker were surely qualified to do, or 'have a go' which one would expect from Foster, who was bowled by Blythe for a duck.

Warwicks had renewed hope when Kent lost two wickets before lunch but on the resumption the pitch had eased, Woolley, 76 in 80 minutes, got after the bowling, to guide to Kent to an unlikely, but brilliant six-wicket victory. Foster, two for 44 in ten overs hardly seemed to make the most of conditions, which surely called for slower pace. Foster had occasionally tossed the ball up with success but here he employed his usual leg-theory with scant results. This result cemented Kent's place atop the table and they won the title. Warwicks on the other hand suffered two dreadful batting collapses in successive matches. And Yorkshire, away were next.

Bramall Lane on a smutty day in front of five thousand Yorkshire supporters would have been pretty daunting to any visiting side but the Tykes' first afternoon collapse from 230 for four to 254 all out, with Foster bowling superbly as usual against his 'second county' to record figures of five for 69 was seen as almost a triumph. *Cricket* reckoned Foster's bowling showed more nip than for sometime past. Unfortunately Warwicks now collapsed to Booth's pace. In their second innings Yorkshire again struggled on a difficult wicket, saved from disaster by Roy Kilner's brilliant 74 in 50 minutes, but Warwicks had little hope of making the required 298 and fell 90 short. Foster was Rhodes' only victim of the match, for 23. Three bad defeats on the trot, Warwicks were surely glad to return to their own midden, where they took on Lancashire, another underachieving side, and in a match of changing fortunes they were thankful to win by two wickets. Foster took seven wickets and played a responsible 60 to steady the ship in the second innings but was twice out to careless shots and put down a 'sitter'.

Gloucestershire now came to Nuneaton. Dipper and Barnett added 113 for the visitors on the first morning but the emerging pace duo of Foster (four for 78) and Jeeves (six for 94) then got to work and later Parsons' maiden century saw Warwicks to a lead of 98. Despite another good innings from Dipper, more fine bowling by Foster, whose four for 50 took his figures to 34 wickets for 666 in five matches and who seemed fully recovered from his domestic collision with a wardrobe, helped his side to an easy win. Any possible new-found optimism was about to be destroyed with the Kent return, just weeks after the Tonbridge debacle. A blank first day mattered little as, for the second successive innings against Warwicks, the sinistral duo of Blythe and Woolley shared ten wickets and Warwicks were dismissed for a slow and unconvincing 159. Kent gained a lead by the close and next day were able to declare 212 on and see their bowlers skittle Warwicks, whose batting *Wisden* summed up as 'feeble'. Warwicks lost by an innings and 51. The skipper's contribution, 0 and 7 and two for 78, was pretty negligible.

Foster, Quaife and Smith now went to Lord's for Gentlemen *v* Players. Batting at eight, Foster was run out for 14 and caused amusement in some quarters in the second innings when he fell for 33, stumped by 'his' Tiger off Barnes. The bare statement tells little however. Single-handed he defied Tarrant and Barnes, who took seven wickets, on what *Wisden* described as a 'ruined' wicket and his 33 was by a deal the highest Gentleman score. He went in at 37 for five and was out at 86 for seven. Foster described his dismissal thus: 'Tiger Smith wangled me out and I laughed like a silly fool. Barnes bowled a ball a little shorter than usual. I pretended to run down the wicket to him, missed it, slipped my right foot back and heard a growl from "my" Tiger of "How's that?" I stood there nonchalantly, told Tiger to shut up, and prepared to take the next ball.' ... '"oppit, skipper. Don't stand there pulling our legs."' The Gentlemen finally succumbed for 102; Foster, it was reported, had never batted better. Not only his single-handed fight was inspirational. R.B.Lagden, a Cambridge Blue but out of his depth here, had amassed one run in his three innings for the Gentlemen this season. On a pair here, he struggled painfully for his first run and owed much to being 'wet-nursed' by Foster. Foster was almost totally ineffective with the ball, a single wicket for 106 in the amateurs' eight-wicket defeat.

Foster's Edgbaston return marked the visit of Derbyshire, in free fall after a promising start and lacking Warren, gone missing, and Chapman, scourge of recent Warwicks attacks. They were led by Tom Forester, ex-Warwicks and Saltley College boy, but after another Parsons century they collapsed twice to Field, with first innings figures of six for 25, and Foster, who had seven for 116 in the match. Now to Old Trafford and a swashbuckling 89 on the first morning by Smith gave hope, but they reckoned without John Tyldesley, who made his eleventh century against Warwicks. The county's batters did fight in their second knock, but Lancashire eventually eased to a seven-wicket win. Scores of one and three, and one wicket for 105 suggest Foster had another of those matches to which he appeared too prone. Bereft of inspiration he seemed of little consequence.

An interesting aside is that in *Cricket* magazine of this time E.H.D.Sewell said Foster had joined Ealing. Despite help from present-day officers of that club no trace has been found of his membership.

The Edgbaston return with struggling Worcestershire gave grounds for optimism, but Foster put them in and lunch saw the visitors 200 for three, with Bowley not out 136, still the best first-morning score in a Warwicks match. He finally reached 177 in 160 minutes but was almost alone and with Foster having figures of six for 76, Worcestershire declined to 266. With Jeeves achieving his best-ever figures of seven for 34 a second innings collapse saw a seven-wicket Warwicks win on the second afternoon. A Yorkshire visit to Edgbaston brought two items of news. Frank Stephens, of the twins, had just been informed a knee injury would not allow him to play again, but the other side of the coin saw a debut for Harry Howell, a square-built local fast bowler of part-Welsh ancestry with some Patagonian thrown in. Howell eventually played for England but was unlucky with his captains, one of whom, A.E.R.Gilligan spent his spare time extolling the virtues of Mussolini's fascism: (Before the 1924/25 tour Special Branch warned its Australian counterpart of the extremist connections of both Gilligan and tour manager Frederick Toone.) The Yorkshire match saw a good effort by Warwicks but a possible victory dash with an even-time half century by Foster was spoiled by rain.

A trip to the Cheltenham Festival was abortive and Surrey must have fancied their Edgbaston chances. They had a fine batting line-up and were facing an attack containing one bowler of uncertain fitness (Field), one whose pace and fire exceeded his control (Howell) and a captain seemingly sick of the game. Although Jeeves took five wickets, a total of 324 must have been disappointing to Surrey. Warwicks' reply of 312 owed nearly all to Quaife and Charlesworth, with contrasting centuries, and Foster's bright 30. Surrey's second-innings tactics were incomprehensible, unless the idea was not to lose. They defended on the third day, reaching 240 for nine in five hours, H.S.Harrison taking 235 minutes over 79, while Ernest Hayes scored 43 in 130 minutes. 'The crowd grew restive' said a report. They finally set a target of 253 in under two hours. One wonders what possessed Surrey skipper Tom Hayward; could his young opposite number not have

Triangular Tournament.
The England team which beat South Africa at Lord's in June 1912 by an innings.
Standing (l to r): W.Brearley, F.E.Woolley, S.F.Barnes, W.Rhodes,
E.Humphreys.
Seated: F.R.Foster, G.L.Jessop, C.B.Fry (capt), P.F.Warner, R.H.Spooner.
On the ground: E.J.Smith (wk), J.B.Hobbs, H.Dean.
Humphreys and Dean were omitted from the final eleven.

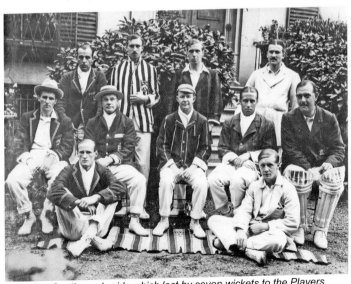

The Gentlemen's side which lost by seven wickets to the Players
at Lord's in July 1913.
Standling (l to r): H.L.Simms, P.G.H.Fender, M.Falcon, E.L.Kidd.
Seated: F.R.Foster, G.L.Jessop, P.F.Warner (capt), J.W.H.T.Douglas,
D.C.Robinson (wk).
On the ground: S.G.Smith, R.B.Lagden.

reminded him about what cricket should mean? Warwicks did try however and reached 179 for five at 5.26 an over. Foster, who made it clear he did not sympathise with Surrey's tactics, opened the batting, posted a quick 25 and he and Smith added 50 in 35 minutes. The best innings though came from Charlesworth. His century came in 70 minutes; no faster hundred has ever been made for Warwicks where runs have not been 'given' in pursuit of a declaration. Quaife, at The Oval, and Charlesworth here, both scored centuries in each innings against Surrey in 1913 – a unique achievement.

Surrey's London rivals Middlesex now came for Edgbaston's final game. Foster won the toss but apart from Quaife his side batted carelessly, their total of 187 being most disappointing. Foster's dismissal – stumped by Joe Murrell off Tarrant – typified the attitude. Middlesex replied with 350 on a deteriorating wicket and Warwicks then collapsed to an innings defeat, and a generally undistinguished Edgbaston season drew to a close.

Two 'out' games remained. Sussex at Hove saw another disappointing effort and a six-wicket beating. Then it was Northampton, scene of the greatest day of Foster's life only two years earlier. Now Northamptonshire were fighting for a top place and Warwicks were also-rans. Unfortunately rain spoiled a pretty even match. Foster at last started taking wickets again, with five for 73 in a long and persistent first-innings spell. As the game began to fade away however, Foster showed that he had given the season up when he gave six overs to young batsman Len Bates, whose bowling was described by a future colleague as resembling a woman turning her arm over under the handicap of too-tight stays. He did however dismiss opposing captain Syd Smith.

The 1913 season saw Warwicks decline from ninth to eleventh, with percentage points slipping from 47.77 to 39.16. They were now on the margins of the 'no-hopers', barely better off than Worcestershire. A county of tiny resources, Northamptonshire, had for the second successive season finished in the top four.

Foster himself had a statistically poorer time than in 1912. In 22 first-class matches he scored 829 runs, av. 23.02, took 92 wickets at 25.48, and held 14 catches. A slight batting improvement was offset by a marked bowling deterioration. The generally better weather certainly affected his record but it is hard to work out how. In Australia the hard wickets had helped him; in 1913 the opposite was suggested, while taking into account more favourable conditions his batting was very similar.

Wisden stated: 'Quite early in the summer Mr F.R.Foster found it necessary to take a rest.' It added: 'Had Foster been the Foster of 1911 the record of the team would, no doubt, have been vastly different. Unfortunately he was not himself. Only now and then did he bowl with his old fire and spin off the pitch, and as a batsman, though he made 111 against Hampshire at Southampton, his aggregate of runs was only 782 and his average 23. The comparative ineffectiveness of his bowling may be judged by the fact that his ninety one wickets cost over twenty four and a half runs each.' The

Almanack referred to the side being handicapped by Kinneir's poor health and Field's injuries, but paid tribute to Jeeves, 'an absolute prize' whose first season 'was nothing short of a triumph.'

Foster declined an invitation to tour South Africa, citing business reasons. He spent another winter with Wilkinson and Riddell but when April came around was probably looking forward to a resumption of his cricket career. He had things to prove. Could he still cut it as a captain? Would the winter's break help him refind the batting capable of destroying any attack, could he regain life and variety with the ball? He was only 25, yet had rarely been regarded as 'young'. Ahead of him – who knew? Even the England captaincy was not simply a wild dream. Or was it?

Whatever cricket fantasies may have been in Frank Foster's mind in the run-up to the 1914 season were now utterly and cruelly shattered. On Friday, 17 April, Frank's beloved father William complained of pain in his head and next day, after going into the city he returned home and took to his bed. Doctors diagnosed pneumonia and on the following Thursday, at 7.15 am, he died at his home.

William Foster had never excelled as a player but from 1910 until his death he had been a member of the Warwicks committee. Only 61, he was in fact survived by both parents, then living in Nuneaton. He was interred at Brandwood End Cemetery, Birmingham and the grave remains in good order in 2010. The service was attended by the family, and by representatives of Moseley Road and Kings Heath Wesleyan Churches, Warwickshire County Cricket Club, the Royal Hackney Society and other equine organisations, and Foster Brothers tailoring. This talented and gregarious man with multifarious interests was given a traditional 'good send-off' but for his son, on the eve of what could be seen as a 'make-or-break' season after two years of disappointment, it was the worst possible situation. He had lost a father he worshipped and since elder brother Harry was unwell and temporarily unable to carry out his duties with Foster Brothers, he decided to retire from first-class cricket, again, and concentrate on the family business. Thankfully he soon changed his mind. Foster had the understanding and support of his family and new company chairman William Webster. This, combined with the clamour from Warwicks fans, among many of whom he had gained icon status, persuaded him to withdraw the proffered resignation as county captain. He would give it one more season; though surely he never imagined the shocking way this statement of intent would come to fruition.[50]

Perhaps it was for the best that Warwicks' season did not commence until 18 May, the opening game at Edgbaston, the opponents the far from

---

50   Only days after William Foster's death another Foster, Reginald Erskine, known as 'Tip', succumbed from 'Type A' diabetes, a killer before the development of insulin. Perhaps the most gifted of the Worcestershire brotherhood (though some plumped for the stage-struck but delicate Basil) and certainly the most successful. Sadly, he and Frank never faced each other in first-class cricket.

formidable Leicestershire. Crockford was the only amateur available – apart from Foster 'a host in himself' according to *World of Cricket*. The campaign could hardly have started better; at lunch Warwicks were 177 without loss, Parsons 97 not out. He fell soon after the break but Kinneir went on to his century, a welcome return to form after his ill-health of 1913. Foster made a carefree 39 but the total of 325 was perhaps a slight let-down. Next day Foster bowled with life and effect, taking five for 69 and when he took the last wicket – Skelding stumped, making a myopic flail – his side had a lead of 129. An aggressive 62 by Smith enabled Foster to declare with a lead of 374 and most of day three remaining and by mid-afternoon Leicestershire had feebly subsided to a 258-run defeat. Foster again finished them off, the ball eluding Skelding's waft on its way to the stumps and his three for 44 was decisive.

The Warwickshire side which beat Leicestershire at Edgbaston in 1914, Foster's last season of big cricket.
Standing (l to r): C.S.Baker, C.Charlesworth, S.Santall, J.H.Parsons, E.F.Field, P.Jeeves.
Seated: S.Kinneir, W.G.Quaife, F.R.Foster (capt), E.B.Crockford, E.J.Smith (wk).

Warwicks may have caught the train to Temple Meads with optimism; a substantial win to start and now to Ashley Down to play Gloucestershire, a shadow of 'the irresistible, the Shire of The Graces long ago'. The Champion now lived, in failing health, in Kent; his brothers, 'the long-whiskered doctor that laugheth rules to scorn' and the much loved G.F., were dead. Charlie Townsend – the Adonis and the greatest spin bowler in the world in his teens – was dispensing law in the north-east and turning out in league cricket for Norton-on-Tees at an age when inferior journeymen are reaching their spinning peak. They now lacked not only G.L.Jessop but local interest. In 1914 they were to win only once; had war not intervened they may not even have survived another season. Excellent bowling by Foster and Hands helped Warwicks to a good lead and then abject Gloucestershire batting meant only 26 was required for a ten-wicket win. A promising start, but not even Foster, optimism renewed, would expect championship aspirants Surrey to roll over as weakly at The Oval.

Little went right. He beat Hayward to the toss and a lunch score of 113 for one seemed promising. The light then deteriorated, an intermittent and depressing drizzle set in, Hitch achieved his only hat-trick and Warwicks collapsed to 226 all out. Matters now went from bad to worse. The weather improved and on the second morning Hobbs moved from 34 to 183 – his 149 runs is the most scored in any pre-lunch session against Warwicks. He hit Foster for 20 in an over, and after the skipper had his revenge, Fender took it out on the demoralised bowlers, racing to 140 in two hours and adding 121 in 45 minutes with W.J.Abel, who himself scored 87 in an hour. Surrey totalled 541, Foster conceding 149 runs in 29 overs for two wickets. On the final day Kinneir and Parsons added 58 for the first wicket after which only Foster, 25 before trying to hoist Abel high to leg showed any fight. The last nine wickets fell for 60, the visitors lost by an innings and 197. A terrible defeat and Foster needed something spectacular in the next game, Worcestershire at Dudley, to restore supporters' faith. He didn't let them down.

Worcestershire won the toss but, though Foster and Jeeves both remained wicketless, a colourless display saw the 'Pear' county subside to 188 in 74.3 overs, leaving Warwicks time to reach 122 for two in 100 minutes by the close. Parsons and Quaife added 116 in 90 minutes before Parsons fell for 102. Quaife was now joined by Foster at 197 for three, and the skipper played with an aggressive assurance none of the bowlers could combat. He reached 50 in 60 minutes, 100 in 105 minutes, 150 in 155 minutes, 200 in 185 minutes. He fairly raced to 250 in 200 minutes – thus adding 50 in 15 minutes – and finally attained the first triple-century by a Warwicks batsman in four hours and ten minutes. When he declared on 305 he had batted 257 minutes. He hit 44 fours and one five but, perhaps surprisingly, no sixes. According to scorer George Austin however, Foster had told him at lunch that he would hit one 'down that bloody chimney' and gestured to Palethorpe's pie and sausage factory at Dudley Port, an impossible hit. Austin claimed Foster did hit a six after lunch but it was not recorded in the scorebook. This was the first instance of a batsman in the Championship scoring 300 or more in a day, and remained a record until 1930, when Duleepsinhji scored 333 in a day for Sussex. Foster remains the only non-specialist batsman to achieve the feat.[51]

---

51   Other statistical highlights include the following points. His 305 not out remains the highest score by a No.5 in any Warwicks match. His 300 was reached in 250 minutes, the quickest by time in any Warwicks match: his closest challengers are I.V.A.Richards, in 276 minutes for Somerset in 1985 and B.C.Lara in 280 minutes against Durham in 1994. His 305 not out was the highest Warwicks score until beaten by Lara's 501* in 1994 and the highest away score until M.A.Wagh scored 315 v Middlesex at Lord's in 2001. At the time Foster's total was the tenth-highest score in English first-class cricket and the seventh-best in the County Championship. It remains the highest score for Warwicks against Worcestershire.

The Warwickshire scorebook, in George Austin's hand, showing Foster's record 305 not out at Dudley in 1914. He hit 44 fours and a five, and scored 305 of the 448 runs added while he was at the wicket.

Contemporary reports stated Foster showed perfect form throughout, giving no semblance of a chance and never being seen to lift the ball until after 200 had been posted. His driving, both off- and on-, was stated to be perfect, and his leg-side play executed with 'wonderful skill and certainty'. He found all the bowling easy, none more so than that of M.K.Foster, whom he hit for 36 in 18 balls. Foster added 126 for the fourth wicket with Quaife, and 166 for the seventh with Tiger Smith. Foster declared at 645 for seven, still Warwicks' best against Worcestershire, but fading light precluded the home side starting their second innings until the third morning.

The delay merely proved to be a stay of execution. The lunch score was 114 for six, and Field quickly polished them off for 136 after the break. Field's figures, 8.4 overs, 7 maidens, 2 runs, 6 wickets remain, statistically speaking, one of the best analyses in the Championship. The skipper was wicketless but one doubts that he cared. An innings and 321 runs was then Warwicks' biggest win, and remains so for an away match.

Championship leaders Middlesex now visited Edgbaston and Foster returned to earth with three in five balls. Rain curtailed play on the second day but Warner could have made a match of it had he shown more enterprise. As it was, Foster showed his feelings by opening the batting and raced to 50 in 15 minutes, at the time the quickest half-century ever in county cricket, still the Warwicks record under genuine conditions and also the fastest for any side against Middlesex. Foster scored 51 of the first 52 runs, allowing Parsons only three balls and was eventually dismissed for

63 out of 71 in 25 minutes. A.R.Litteljohn took his wicket after being hit for four sixes in 11 balls: he must have been glad of a medical career on which to fall back. A day's break and Warwicks travelled to Lord's for the return. Warwicks batted first in poor light and J.W.Hearne, now 23, emphasised the value of youthful enterprise in a spinner, posting figures of eight for 117. Middlesex, from whose side it was rumoured P.F.Warner had been dropped, gained first-innings lead which was compounded when in light described as 'yellowish-grey' Warwicks collapsed against Tarrant's spin to 69 all out. In suddenly improved conditions, Middlesex comfortably scored the required 25 runs for victory.

Derbyshire at Edgbaston, a win essential if 1914 was not already to be a write-off. Warwicks' 180 began to look reasonable when Derbyshire lost three for 9, six for 30, and ten for 71. Foster and Field bowled unchanged and were irresistible. Foster twice took two in two balls and figures of six for 18 in 18 overs were a fair indication of his form, while Field, four for 36, supported well. Finally given a day to score 253, Derbyshire skipper Capt R.R.C.Baggallay, in first to show the troops how things should be done, soon fell to Howell who, bowling very fast, achieved figures of six for 31 and the visitors, all out 127, made no show.

Foster's batting had gone off the boil but there was disquiet at a statement in the magazine *World of Cricket* issued on 26 June: 'Frank Foster is evidently of a retiring disposition. It is said he will retire from county cricket at the end of this season. Seriously we hope not. Warwickshire could ill afford to lose him.' The magazine felt he did not really mean it; suggestions of 'crying wolf' were implicit in the language used. Perhaps Foster was 'simply' depressed again.

He needed to be in the right frame of mind for the next game – Yorkshire at Dewsbury – and a brilliant 206 by Charlesworth enabled Foster to declare on the second morning at 424 for eight. A team effort saw Yorkshire dismissed for 262. Foster happily enforced the follow-on but consistent batting enabled the Tykes to declare at 345 for nine, setting a victory target of 184 at nearly three a minute. Foster's tactics had been puzzling; he opened the bowling with Quaife and Hands and gave himself only five overs and Field ten. Sending himself in first, Foster made a token effort, racing to 38 out of 63, before the game petered out to a disappointing draw. Things were easier when winless Gloucestershire now visited the Bull's Head ground at Coventry and more fine batting by Charlesworth, 115 in 100 minutes, and excellent bowling by Field and Foster left the visitors with a day and a half to save the game. All out 94 was not the way to do it: they batted spinelessly. Howell was lethal and even Jessop scrambled singles to keep himself away from the youngster.

There was now a break for the Lord's 'Centenary Game' and it almost defied belief that Foster was not chosen. George Hirst, a shadow of his old self, was there as was the tyro George Geary, a reward for a good spell at Lord's a couple of weeks earlier. One wonders at Foster's feelings at being ignored for so historic an event. Lancashire came to Edgbaston and it being

Sep Kinneir's benefit he picked the team. For no reason now apparent he preferred Hands to Howell. The beneficiary chose to bat and calamity ensured – he was caught behind for two. Only an aggressive 56 in an hour by Foster, and a subdued 83 from Baker enabled Warwicks to reach 222. That this was insufficient was due almost entirely to a great 156 by Ernest Tyldesley and a last wicket stand of 131 with Ralph Whitehead. Lancashire registered a lead of 103. Warwicks' impressive second innings owed much to Kinneir, who had the mortification of being dismissed for 98 in his benefit match, and Foster, who joined him at 28 for one and, when dismissed 40 minutes later, had scored 83 of the 101 added. Foster reached his fifty in 25 minutes placing him second, to himself, among Warwicks' fast half-century scorers. Set to chase 293 in more than two sessions Lancashire never showed the slightest predisposition for a fight and were 100 for nine, with plenty of time left, when a torrential downpour saved them. Foster's figures were five for 19 in 14 overs, Quaife's four for 16 in eight. Match statistics of 139 in 100 minutes, and six for 83, yet Foster had been cheated of a win. Rubbing salt in the wounds, Lancashire went away with three points for first-innings lead, Warwicks only one. Rain and defensive tactics by Sussex cancelled out another good allround effort by Foster – five for 72 and 60 in 75 minutes in the following match and he maintained form against Hants at Edgbaston. After taking six for 63 in 27 overs Foster joined Quaife at 38 for three. Quaife scored eight of their stand of 42 and Foster raced to 75 out of 102 in 65 minutes. With Foster and Jeeves taking five each in Hampshire's second knock, Warwicks eased to a seven-wicket win: 75 and 23 not out and 11 wickets for 141 – yet another outstanding performance.

Sussex at Hastings clashed with The Oval's Gentlemen *v* Players fixture. Parsons and Jeeves appeared for the Players but Foster preferred to lead his county. Sadly Warwicks were quite outplayed though, when set 394 to win, Foster set the right example, opening the innings and firing a quick 45 in a stand of 63, but a 259-run defeat saw the visitors emerge with little credit. Back to Lord's for the Gentlemen *v* Players; great bowling by Johnny Douglas sent the professionals plunging to a heavy defeat and Foster gave good support with bat and ball. Warwicks now journeyed to Northampton; Foster batted and bowled with aggression but set to score 306 in 210 minutes, fell for 29 out of 35 and the shutters were put up.

Two days later, and the Northamptonshire return and the 'interesting' selection of Foster's younger brother Arthur, a Cambridge soccer Blue and Birmingham F.C. forward but with no track record as a cricketer. Having suffered a hand injury, Smith played as a batsman and Arthur Foster kept wicket. According to Frank, he had to persuade him to play 'although he wasn't much good'. He told him to stand guarding middle and leg, not to move his feet and just sway on his toes to right or left, so if his hands missed the ball it would hit his body. The game itself was played in doleful weather and remained unfinished, with Arthur taking two catches, neither off Frank's bowling, and conceding fifteen byes. It was notable only for Syd Smith's taking four wickets with four balls, still unique for Edgbaston. One of the four was Arthur, his first ball in first-class cricket; second time around he did better and was unbeaten on one when the game was abandoned.

Another damp draw followed, against Leicestershire at Hinckley; Warwicks were grateful for a gritty century from Kinneir – his last. But Foster and his side now had a happier time at the only first-class match ever played at Lancaster. Quaife and Baker scored centuries; then Foster (four for 58) and Jeeves (six for 51) skittled Lancashire for 128. Foster, 'stumped by a mile' off Dean for 14 declared to set Lancashire a target of 361, or playing out the last day. They did neither; Foster creamed off the four top men and Lancashire were well beaten. The match finished with Ralph Whitehead run out trying to 'steal' the bowling. That incident alone summed up the worst-ever season for the Red Rose.

Foster had no clue as he led out his men at the start of August for the Edgbaston return with Worcestershire that this was to be his last local derby; he would certainly not have anticipated an incident involving one of the 'other' Fosters. In miserable weather the visitors collapsed to 122 all out, Jeeves taking seven for 52 and Foster three for 50, his wickets including Geoffrey and Neville Foster. Warwicks replied, amidst interruptions, with 139 all out. There was little to play for, but Worcestershire could hardly have wished to slump to 14 for four before the game was called off. The match was dead yet M.K.Foster regarded it as of sufficient importance to make a name for himself, albeit in entirely the wrong way.

Worcestershire had made a dire start and when Maurice Foster joined Bowley they were 7 for three and Frank Foster had just dismissed 'Spinney' Lane.[52] Maurice Foster came to the wicket and played the last ball of the over, for no run. Jeeves bowled a maiden to Bowley and Foster (M.K.) now faced Foster (F.R.) again. The first ball was reported to have bowled him 'neck and crop' but instead of quietly departing like the great sportsmen the Worcester Fosters supposedly were, he refused to leave the crease, claiming he was 'not ready'. When Smith passed on the message to Frank Foster his reputed reaction was 'Not ready? Here, throw me the ******* ball, Tiger.' He then bowled what Smith reckoned was the fastest ball Foster ever sent down, pitching full toss on top of the stumps with the batsman doing a rapid backward chassé towards square leg. 'Now will you go?' Frank shouted down the pitch to Maurice, who did as he was asked, having been

---

52   'Spinney' Lane, an ebullient Black Country character, was in his first season, apparently as a professional. In a curious career Lane played for Warwicks as an amateur from 1919 to 1925 then returned to Worcestershire, for whom he last played in 1932 aged 46. A self-made industrialist, Lane was awarded an M.B.E. for his services to the First World War arms industry. In the Second World War he worked hard organising cricket in the Birmingham area.

dismissed twice in two balls by the opposing skipper.[53]

Something more sinister – neither Geoffrey nor Neville Foster was able to bat in the second innings, both having been called to their regiment. As the Foreign Office statement issued on 4 August bluntly put it: ' ... His Majesty's Government have declared to the German Government that a state of war exists between Great Britain and Germany as from 11 pm.' The shades were lengthening on a world which ended with the forthcoming hostilities, and the next opponents, Yorkshire, had their captain, Sir Archie White, reporting for action. It was a disappointing match; left to score 260 to win with plenty of time available, Foster decided to open and fired a quick 43 but once he departed 67 for three soon became 96 all out. Happily Derbyshire, on a treacherous Derby wicket, proved less of a problem. Foster and the veteran Santall each took five first-innings wickets, Jeeves and Foster, with four apiece did the second innings damage. A target of 115 in a day and a half should have been a formality, but Warwicks slumped to 56 for four. The skipper came to the rescue however, scoring 48 of a winning fifth-wicket stand of 59 with Quaife. Nine wickets and more runs than anyone on either side; a captain's victory.

An inexperienced leg spinner of about 5ft 2in got the county's next match, with Kent, off to the worst of starts. Flighting cleverly and spinning seductively, 'Tich' Freeman had the batsmen all at sea and took seven for 25 in ten overs to have Warwicks all out 111 before lunch on the first morning. Foster's 28 was brief but merry but only Kinneir, ninth out for 31 showed Freeman the necessary respect. County batsmen unwilling to use their feet would have enough trouble from Freeman after the war but here his success was unexpected. On a beast of a pitch Kent matched the Warwicks score exactly, but Warwicks were again dismissed before the close of the first day and in easier conditions on the second morning Kent posted a nine-wicket victory.

Portsmouth was to be the venue for the following match but the international situation saw it transferred to Southampton. A brilliant 92 in 95 minutes by Foster saved his side from serious harm but Hampshire had the better of an even game, winning by four wickets after Foster gave himself only six late overs. Along to Canterbury, and another first day full of action; Foster and Field had four wickets apiece as they sent Kent packing for 167 but there was sufficient first-day time left to see Warwicks too, all out, for 179, their slender lead due almost wholly to a whirlwind 61 in 50 minutes from Jeeves. Fiery bowling by Foster, who had figures of five

53 The main details of this story came from Tiger Smith in old age, and Leslie Deakins, long time Warwicks secretary. It is an interesting comment on county cricket in another age. Maurice Foster did what he did because he knew he could get away with it. Doubtless he did not fancy a second cheap dismissal. The umpires were Harry Bagshaw, ex-Derbyshire, and William Phillips, a comparative tyro from Lancashire, a Test umpire in 1921 but who later disappeared from the scene so completely that nothing is known of his later life. Reappointment to the first-class list was vital. They could not afford to get on the wrong side of so influential a family.

for 53 in 26 overs gave Warwicks a realistic victory target of 199 but, Foster falling first ball, they were a disappointing 100 runs short.

And so to Warwicks' final match, on 27, 28 and 29 August, and Frank Foster's last-ever for them. The venue Edgbaston, champions-elect Surrey the opposition. He could not possibly know what was to happen, yet perhaps he may have sensed that here, too, was his own parting of the ways. He would surely have thought it ominous that Collin Langley had to leave on the second day to report to his regiment, the Honourable Artillery Company. 'At least they play cricket there', Foster claimed to have said to Langley. 'No Frank, this is more serious than cricket.' War wounds meant Langley was never able to play top cricket again – though his services to Warwicks were noble, albeit perhaps unappreciated in 2011.

Winning the toss, Foster decided to open. He hit the first ball for four and was out for a superb 81 out of 120 before lunch. The quality of Foster's innings may be measured by the fact that Quaife achieved a typical 60 in 150 minutes, but third-highest scorer was Tiger Smith with 9, the total a mere 177. Surrey now demonstrated the hardships batsmen faced as they limped to 126 all out. Few had an answer to Foster's pace and swerve as he dismissed the stylish but limpet-like D.J.Knight, Fender, Abel and 'Razor' Smith in 16.2 overs for only 24 runs. Jeeves, another last-match man (albeit unbeknown to him) was even more incisive with figures of five for 52. Warwicks' second innings was low key. By now, the first wounded British troops were being landed at Folkestone and some players seemed merely to go through the motions. Foster again opened and achieved one of his most sedate innings ever – for seven runs. No innings of merit was played in a total of 159, though Jeeves did score 18 in 12 balls. He never again held a bat in anger.[54]

Requiring 211, Surrey finished the second day 41 for three, Ducat and Hayes together and would perhaps have been regarded as favourites. Frank Foster would not have backed them. Surrey made a steady start on the third morning; no hurry, they could stroll to victory. At 84 Ernest Hayes was run out for 23. Six runs later Ducat gave Jeeves his last first-class wicket. Foster now got to work. He bowled Fender for 14, (111 for six) then Howell dismissed 'B'litch' (118 for seven). The rest was all Foster. He bowled 'Razor' Smith for a duck (119 for eight), then William Abel and Strudwick had a stubborn stand of 11 before Foster, in his twenty-eighth over, dug into what was left of his reserves and bowled Abel and Rushby with successive balls. Warwicks had inflicted only the second defeat of the season on the champions but at the distance of nearly 100 years this seems rather by the way. Foster took wickets, both bowled, with what were his last two balls in first-class cricket. His innings figures were five for 48 from 27.4 overs. More to the point he had rounded things off with a spell of 18.4 overs for 38 runs and five wickets. A quickfire 81, nine wickets for 72, and

54   A private with the 'Birmingham Pals', Jeeves died at Montauban, France in July 1916. His body was never found. His name was of course P.G.Wodehouse's inspiration for Bertie Wooster's 'gentleman's gentleman.'

an unlikely victory. More runs and wickets than any other player for either side. The last seven Surrey wickets fell on the third morning for 49. As *Wisden* later said 'Surrey ought at least to have made a close fight.' *Wisden* and Surrey reckoned without Frank Foster.

The whole thing was surreal; in all the circumstances no plot devised by man could have had a more appropriate, more romantic, more tear-jerking finale. Perhaps it should end here; from now it was all downhill, into depths of unbelievable trauma, a fall to which no human being should be subjected.

Chapter Eight
War and the 1920s

The start of the Great War brought changes of such a huge scale to the lives of so many people that it was sometimes described by many of the more leisured classes as the end of their world. Tough. This writer's grandfathers were working in the South Staffs coalfield in 1900, still there in 1914, again when the armistice was signed in 1918. Not much changed for them. Frank Foster's life certainly changed however, but only partly and indirectly because of the war.

Naturally a number of Warwicks players obeyed the call. Jack Parsons was so keen to do the right thing that he called at the Foster house in his Territorial Army uniform to seek advice. He was impressed at the opulence of the place, and taken aback by the servants on hand to see to every whim of the Foster family, but the attitude of Frank Foster disappointed him. Foster apparently took exception to his even wearing his 'Terriers' uniform, pointing out he was still being paid by the County Club, not the Army. Unabashed, Parsons joined the Warwickshire Yeomanry, was eventually commissioned, had a distinguished war and in later years became an Anglican clergyman, the only first-class professional cricketer ever to change careers in that way. Frank Foster professed to believe in God: there the similarities seemed to end. Incidentally this attitude towards the war is somewhat surprising since Birmingham raised three battalions and Foster Brothers clothed two of them, as well as making nosebags for the French Cavalry. The company and, indirectly Frank, did all right out of the horrific conflict.

There is, though, a mystery over what Frank Foster actually did in the war. Brother Harry, presumably because he was running the family business (but also perhaps due to health problems), did not serve, but brother Edgar did his bit while other brother Arthur was also commissioned early on. Of wars, Arthur's grew 'curiouser and curiouser.' A lieutenant at the outset, when finally released from the glasshouse in 1920 he was a private. A serial deserter he was in and out of prison, and never left British shores, which maybe explains why he was never shot, since no-one better deserved such a fate. Arthur's service record also reveals the presence of two sexually transmitted diseases. This appalling man showed no improvement in lifestyle later on; even now some of the damage he did is remembered with disdain by those affected. Then there is Frank.

The Solihull School magazine for March 1915 states that he was a lieutenant in the Public Schools Battalion of the Royal Fusiliers, but I have traced no record of this in official sources. In any event whether or not he joined up became academic when on 12 August 1915 he was motor-cycling in Barbourne Road, Worcester, at the time the town's main exit for anyone wishing to travel by road to Birmingham. In order to avoid a collision with an electric lamp standard – another version suggests it was an electric tram – he crashed to the ground so heavily that he received a compound fracture of the lower right leg. He was attended by a medical officer from the Voluntary Aid Detachment and taken home by car. This sounds extraordinary since, according to his family, only the fact that he was a young and physically fit sportsman stopped his foot being amputated. In any event his career in major cricket was over.[55]

Naturally there were many visitors to his home, and one of those was Margaret, young daughter of R.V.Ryder. She said how thrilled she was when her father took her along to Foster's bedside: 'When the talk was finished and we moved to leave, Mr Foster called me back and gave me a box of chocolates.' The minutes of a the County Club's committee for 9 September expressed sympathy and ordered a letter to be sent, hoping he would soon resume his activities. There was never a hope.

Foster's accident and dire injuries did seem to have an upside. On 13 October 1915, at St Agnes Church, Moseley, he married Norah Gladys Pritchard, a 25-year-old nurse from a Welsh family. Her address was given as Mel Valley, the same as her groom and his family. She certainly nursed him through his injuries but it has not been established whether they were known to each other previously. The marriage was not to last, but did produce three children David William, John Pritchard and Elizabeth ('Tiz').[56]

Foster knew his first-class career was over when, in January 1919, he suggested to the County Club that he be made team manager at a salary of £1,000 per year. The idea was not adopted and the following month it was announced that due to his foot injury he would be unable to play. His resignation as captain was accepted by the committee 'with regret' but he was appointed to a committee vacancy. The appointment, though on the face of it justified, was not a success. A classic case of an 'absentee' committee member, and so far as can be ascertained no official regret was expressed when he resigned his seat on 18 July 1922. This talented, impulsive, effervescent man was never likely to be happy on a committee; as his life and mental health began to collapse, things would have become impossible. He ought never to have been there in the first place, but got out at the right time. Despite now having no active role, Foster was still highly regarded and in 1926 he was offered, and accepted, an honorary life membership.

Despite Foster's inaction on the Warwicks committee he was still remembered and highly regarded in the cricket world at large. Why else

---

55 A legend exists that, for many years afterwards, the wreck of the motor cycle was displayed somewhere in the Chad Valley district of Birmingham.
56 See Appendix Two.

would a Warwickshire newspaper, *The Observer*, have commissioned an article entitled 'Cricket Fitness' under his name for its 9 July 1920 issue? The reader is told that natural talent notwithstanding, it is best if a cricketer gets himself fit and stays keen. Such stating of the obvious, and so unmemorable is it in both style and content, one wonders whether Foster did any more than put his name to the article.

Lest it seem that his post-accident career was spent in idleness, this was not the case – at least not officially. When Foster's father died in 1914, W.T.Webster, having been joint managing director of Foster Brothers became the sole managing director. Elizabeth Foster, Frank's mother became the company chairman and, on Webster's death in 1918, Harry Foster, Frank's oldest brother took over as managing director. Meanwhile another brother, Edgar, with two others, gave practical help with the day-to-day running of the business and in 1936 Edgar became a director. The remaining brothers, Frank and Arthur, also became employees of the company – nominally at least. Frank was superintendent of ten shops, for which he was paid £4,000 per annum.[57] He also owned £5,000 of shares in 1921, subsequently given to his mother in return for which she cleared gambling debts for him. Given Foster Brothers' success this was Frank's big chance, but he blew it. In 1928 he left the firm – for reasons unspecified – but was granted an annual allowance of £2,000. This was reduced to £1,400 in 1930 when his marriage broke up. Serious cricket was of course out of the question, but he is believed to have turned out in various 'scratch' matches involving 'Foster' teams, once at least with his son David.

During the years from 1914, Frank seemed to change his address with regularity. In 1914 he is found at 'Innesscrone', Stratford Road, Hall Green, and after his wedding at 'Tralee', Woodlands Road, Moseley, just a short distance from the family home, Mel Valley. Later he and his wife were living at Lode Lane, Solihull, but they then seem to have returned to Mel Valley. This would appear to have been a mixed blessing for Frank's mother. The drinking sprees there of Frank and brother Arthur became a family legend; on at least one occasion their mother begged eldest son Harry to go and sort things out, since she feared that the drunken brawl in which they were involved would result in damage to her home, and serious injury to themselves. In the 1920s Arthur Foster was also supposedly employed by the family business but seems to have done no work. He began selling motor cars and was a notorious womaniser, despite being married and having sexually transmitted diseases. He could almost have been a model for the unlikeable rogue Jack Favell in Daphne du Maurier's *Rebecca*.

As the 1920s went by, Frank Foster paid only lip service to the responsibilities of being a husband, a father, and a business executive. The following, which appears to have been written by Foster himself, and intended for inclusion in the unpublished second volume of his memoirs,

---

57   The equivalent of £84,000 at 2011 values, surely an extraordinary amount in the early 1920s.

gives a fair indication of the sort of life he was leading and the deterioration of his mind:

> Time: Early morning of Derby Day, 1927. Place: Bureau of a well known London hotel. Characters: My best friend in that hotel – night porter Robert Newman, the late Walter Griggs, the racehorse trainer, myself. Action: FRF propping up the counter, discussing with the night porter, over a night-cap, the possible result of the Derby, to take place later in the day. In walks the 'Acme of Perfection' in evening dress, goes across to the covered sandwiches, removes the lid and commences to devour sandwich after sandwich.

> 'Hungry?' said I, smiling wickedly.
> 'Umph!' replies Acme, 'not so bad.'
> He then proceeds to help himself to more sandwiches, with an 'ell of a twinkle' in his eye.
> 'What – what's going to win the Derby?' I stuttered.
> 'Hot Night,' he stammered.
> 'Lord loves us,' I said, 'but surely a call-boy never had a hot night. I will lay you 10 to 1 against your dud.'
> 'Done,' said he.
> I take another sip of my night-cap and then offer 8 to 1.
> 'Taken,' said he.
> I look at Robert and my friend winks. Mistaking the wink I offer 7 to 1.
> 'That's enough,' said the sandwich king as he passed £3 to my pal behind the counter, and so he went to bed.
> 'Do you know who that is?' said Robert.
> 'No,' I replied.
> 'Well, that is Walter Griggs, the trainer,' murmured the N.P. The nightcap having now gone the way of all nightcaps I make the best of the situation and retire to my couch with the feeling I shall be minus a 'pony' before W.G. partakes of his next sandwich.

> On the morning of the great day (after a little sleep) a friend rang me up on the phone. I was then emerging from a state of coma, and the following conversation ensued:
> 'Coming on the Pullman, Frank?' 'No,' I replied, 'I go by road.'
> 'You will never get there,' he said. 'Good enough Walter,' I rambled, 'my book is closed, 25 to 3 is quite enough gambling for me.' (I thought for the moment my friend was eating sandwiches.)
> 'Is that you Billy dear?' murmured a sweet voice over the wire. 'No!' said I, 'my name is Rothschild, and my middle name is Rowbotham.' 'Ring off!' she screamed, 'you are not quite the thing.' The lady was perfectly correct, I felt like it.

> Racing began at 1.30, the second race 2.30. I decided to miss the first event and took my departure from the very centre of London in a taxi, all by myself, at 12.30.

We, the driver and myself, arrived outside that marvellous new stand at Epsom at exactly 1.39, without one single stop. The weather was perfect and the day was – Derby Day. There is no need for me to enlarge on 'How to get there.' The press gave all the details, on the morning of 'Frank Curzon's Day'.[58] With your kind permission we will now move the scene of action to the racecourse, where the parade of candidates for the big race is about to commence. This is my first Derby, and the sight is truly wonderful. Picture me now seated on my reserved seat in the stand, watching the parade. On my one side a dear old lady sits (not a dear young lady) dressed à la Epsom. On my other side fidgets the Acme of Perfection in morning attire – not Walter I am sorry to say.
'What have you backed?' the lady said to me.
'Call Boy,' I replied.
'So have I,' she murmured, 'and I have taken 6 to 1 for my five shillings. I do hope he wins, don't you?' As I considered that remark in the light of a leading question, I confided to the lady, in hurried whispers, my foolish bet made in the early hours of the morning.
'They're off!''she exclaimed, with a cheery 'Good luck' thrown in.

Up went our glasses (not night caps) and after a few yards we saw Elliott[59] take Call Boy to the front. 'He leads,' the lady said. 'Thank you,' I replied as my glasses were not too clear – you will notice the glass takes all blame. Round Tattenham Corner this 'nice 'oss' was still in the lead. A furlong from home I drop my glasses and exclaim, 'He's beat.' At that moment Hot Night, lying second, reached the girths of Call Boy and to me, a novice at the game, it looked as if Hot Night was going to win.

'Stop him!' I shouted. The next moment I felt a pair of warm, bare arms around my neck, and my lady friend of the next pew to mine uttered these soul-stirring words: 'Look, you fool, he's won, he's won.' And so he had. When I dropped my glasses the effort of Hot Night had reached its climax and it was Call Boy that went on to win that wonderful race.'

The following year Foster Brothers Limited dispensed with Frank's services though, as mentioned, he was given a pretty generous pay-off and the summer, at least, was spent in Bournemouth, where he became involved with Bournemouth Cricket Club. Though not a regular member of the Bournemouth eleven he did play occasionally and left a good, though perhaps hyperbolic description of a game in July against an MCC side at Dean Park:

I should like to tell you something about one of the finest amateur bowlers I have ever seen. His name, Bostock-Hill, is not very well known, because the Warwickshire club did not think he was much good. I saw this man put up one of the finest bowling performances

---

58   Frank Curzon was a well known theatre manager and horse breeder whose horse, Call Boy, won the 1927 Derby.
59   Charlie Elliott (1904-79) shared the Jockeys Championship with Steve Donohue in 1923, while still an apprentice.

seen in club cricket in 1928, and the match was played on the County Ground at Bournemouth. We were both playing for Bournemouth against MCC. It was a two-day match, and MCC had sent a very strong side for the occasion. General Poore[60] was in charge of the MCC, and here is a nice spicy bit of news. Bournemouth lost the toss, and General Poore walked into bat at the fall of the second wicket. A fast bowler was bowling, I was fielding second slip. Suddenly the General cut one hard, wide of my right hand. The ball caught the top of the nail of my middle finger. As quick as lightning I moved my right arm upwards and clenched my fingers. The catch was made, but my nail was badly damaged. At that time, General Poore had not scored. I quickly put the ball in my pocket and sucked my injured nail. Then, I looked up expecting to see the General walking towards the pavilion. Nothing of the sort, he was half-way up the wicket (I could have run him out easily) arguing the point with the umpire. The umpire gave him not out because Poore told him it was a 'bump ball.' After this bit of umpire bullying General Poore proceeded to make a priceless 70 runs.

In the second innings of MCC the bowler I began to tell you about, Bostock-Hill, clean bowled the General for a duck. I was fielding short square leg. 'Now what's going to happen?' I said to myself. General Poore walked up the wicket and pointed with his bat to the dense mass of trees behind the bowlers arm. 'How's that?' someone shouted. 'Out,' said the umpire. It was a different umpire that innings. As the General passed me he said, 'I never saw the damn ball.' 'Why don't you go back and tell the umpire?' I replied. The General smiled and walked sadly away to the pavilion.

The Bournemouth wicket is treacherous after rain followed by bright sunshine, but that did not mean such a lot to Bostock-Hill.[61] Although he captured seven wickets for 20 runs (after six in the first innings) he did not experience the best of luck. He should have captured all ten wickets for less than ten runs if our fielding had been up to scratch. I have never seen a bowler that so closely resembles my old pal Sydney Barnes in every department since 1914. They are about the same height, they both possess long arms and long fingers and they are both able to make the ball turn either way without any noticeable change of action. Warwickshire made a big mistake in not encouraging Bostock-Hill to play regularly for the club, just in the same way that they did not encourage Sydney Barnes to stay in the County when he was a member of the groundstaff. Warwickshire let two of the finest bowlers anyone will ever see slip through their fingers. Mistakes are

---

60   Robert Montague Poore had a fearsome reputation as both cricketer and man. In 1899 his 12 first-class matches, for Hants and others, brought him 1,551 runs, av. 91.23. When asked years later how he would play Larwood he is reputed to have roared 'I would charge him, Sir!'

61   Alfred John Bostock Hill did play once for Warwicks in 1920, with little success, but he was a career diplomat and spent much of the 1920s and 1930s in the Far East, playing cricket with great success in Malaya and Hong Kong. Two uncles, J.E. and H.B.G.Hill had played for Warwicks in the 1890s.

made by everyone but I think the above errors were the biggest ever made by a County Cricket Club.[62]

Foster reported that he had not played cricket since 1928, but 'for two solid months' in that year he says he had some 'wonderful experiences'. He continued:

> After a few matches with Bournemouth I was invited to play for Sir John Power's XI.[63] He had a beautiful house with his own cricket ground attached, not very far from Bournemouth. The first game I played there was for Bournemouth. I got Sir John out twice lbw. The following morning he button-holed me about 11 o'clock and said: 'Will you give me a demonstration after today's play of how a left-arm bowler round the wicket can get a batsman out lbw? We tried it out on the billiards table last night with matches for stumps and tape for lines. There is only an inch or two to spare for a bowler of your description to get an lbw decision. I looked at Sir John and this was my reply, 'I think you have forgotten one thing.' 'What's that?' he rapped out. 'Well, Sir John, if a left-arm bowler bowling round the wicket pitches the ball practically on the front foot of the batsman, with the seam upwards, and that ball straightens itself the batsman must be out if the ball hits his pad instead of the wicket.' There was no demonstration that evening!

Foster also left his feelings about other matters respecting cricket in Hampshire in his unpublished notes:

> The secretary of Bournemouth Cricket Club was C. Garnet Fynn, one of the best googly bowlers I have ever seen. I watched him closely for two solid months and in January 1929 I sent a letter to Plum Warner giving full details of his bowling. Fynn was Middlesex-qualified by birth, Hampshire by residence, but unfortunately decided to play for Hampshire, in my opinion a sad error. Hampshire have always been noted for their absolute snobbishness and had my friend played for Middlesex he would have had far better treatment.

> I have a decided axe to grind so I will grind it. If it had not been for me, Fynn would never have played for any county club and I think I am in a position to express my opinion on the whole matter. The first county match my friend played in for Hampshire he obtained two wickets in his very first over. Lord Tennyson is a very funny man and, after the treatment he meted out to Fynn, I am downright ashamed of him. I

---

62   I have obtained the scorecard of the MCC match described and although Foster's memory is a little faulty he is basically correct. The score summarised is MCC 260 (R.M.Poore 81, A.J.Bostock-Hill six wkts) and 54 (A.J.Bostock-Hill 7 wkts; R.M.Poore lbw Bostock Hill 1); Bournemouth 189 (G.W.Parker 93, F.R.Foster 1) and 110 (F.R.Foster 7). C.G.Fynn did not take a wicket. Two weeks later Foster played for Bournemouth against The Frogs. Frogs won but in what was probably his last organised match, Foster, after being caught and bowled for a duck, took five of the seven wickets to fall in The Frogs' only innings.
63   Power lived at Yeatton House, Hordle, near Lymington in Hampshire in this period, and at the time he was Conservative MP for Wimbledon.

know exactly what passed through the Hampshire captain's mind when Charlie Fynn got those two wickets in his first over. This was it. 'My God this man *is* a bowler. What am I going to do with my mainstays, Newman, Kennedy and so on?'

This is what happened. In match after match poor old Charlie Fynn was put in the long field for hour after hour and when thoroughly tired out he was asked to bowl. I ask you, is it fair to put a googly bowler, of all people, in the deep for hours and hours without giving him a bowl? It decidedly is not. If Charlie Fynn had not got fed up and refused to play he would have been the finest googly bowler in England [1933] if he had played for Middlesex. Fynn was much faster off the pitch than Robins, bowled a better length and his 'wrong un' was far more deceptable. [*sic*]. I don't care a bit what anybody says. I have seen Robins (in 1933) and I saw Fynn in 1928, so there is no argument.[64]

---

64   Fynn played as an amateur in seven first-class matches for Hampshire in 1930 and two in 1931, scoring in all 45 runs at 6.42 and taking eleven wickets, many of them top-class batsmen, at 40.54.

Chapter Nine
The shambolic 1930s

It is uncertain how long Foster remained in Bournemouth, but what is undeniable is that in 1931 he was living in a luxury flat in Ryder Street, St. James in the heart of London gentlemen's club land. It seems likely he was residing in London, at least temporarily, in late 1929, as the following sad story would seem to suggest.

Early on 2 October 1931 the body of Annie Louise Norah Upchurch, a twenty-year-old prostitute, was found strangled in an empty shop on the corner of Shaftesbury Avenue and Old Compton Street, in Soho, around the corner from where she lived and plied her trade. A cheque was found in her flat, signed by Foster. In the ensuing coroner's court case, Foster told the court that he first met Miss Upchurch two years earlier in Pimlico and, taking pity on her hungry and frightened appearance, he accompanied her, at her request, to her home. She refused to tell him why she was frightened and when he went to leave she begged him to stay. She stated she owed £10: there is no evidence Foster gave her money in this instance, but perhaps one can surmise.

Foster said that she had dozed and he sat quietly in a chair in the dark. He then heard a 'curious' noise. He stated that a street lamp outside lit up both the window and the door. He swore no-one had entered the room by window or door yet suddenly a man appeared as if from nowhere at the girl's bedside. Foster reckoned there must have been a secret panel or hidden door. 'I am certain that if this man can be found he would be able to throw a good deal of light on the death of Nora Upchurch,' Foster reckoned. He said that when he asked Norah Upchurch about the man she told him nothing.

This unlikely sounding story now moves on to 28 September 1931. Foster met the girl, known to him as Norah Laverick, outside Piccadilly Circus tube station (clearly by prior arrangement) at 8 pm and after they had dined at the Garrick Grill Room he took her by taxi to his flat. There he picked up a bottle of whisky, a hundred cigarettes and some playing cards, part payment he claimed for the night of 'entertainment', since, as he explained to the prostitute, he had little ready money. They then went to her place in Warwick Street and he claimed he spent the night sleeping in an arm-chair. He also gave her a cheque for £10 after she told him she had urgent debts. 'I tried to help her you see.' The coroner, Mr Ingleby Oddie, then commented 'You did not help her very much by giving her a "dud" cheque.' Foster replied that he had been expecting money. Foster left the following morning. That evening, however, Foster was listening to a 'religious

*Ryder Street, St James in 2010.
Foster lived here in the early
1930s.*

meeting' in Leicester Street when he saw Norah plying her trade. He did not speak to her and she did not see him. The coroner remarked that it was as well that she failed to see him since the cheque had been returned that afternoon marked 'Refer to Drawer', there being no funds in Foster's account. Asked if he had ever been to the shop where the girl was found, or had a key, he replied in the negative. He said the first he knew of the murder was when he read about it on 3 October. When he was shown a photograph of the dead girl he recognized her.

Also in court was one Frederick Field, a sign fixer, who claimed he had been engaged to do some work at the empty shop. He then handed over the shop key to 'a man in a plus-four suit', who subsequently 'disappeared'. Field was cautioned and sent for trial, but nothing was proven against him. As a postscript, in April 1936, Field, by now an airman stationed at Hendon, was convicted of murdering 48-year-old Beatrice Sutton. Before being sent to the gallows he confessed to having murdered Norah Upchurch.

So, if Field's confession is accepted, Frank Foster was innocent of murder, but could the word of a notorious liar and fantasist be necessarily true? He had nothing to lose, so why not become even more famous by claiming to be a double, rather than single, murderer? Revelations during the case showed the low life to which Foster had sunk; the fact that a £10 cheque bounced said much for his financial situation. He no longer lived in the real world and would have been capable of anything.

Foster was not quite finished with cricket however. In 1932, Douglas Jardine was asked to take the MCC tourists to Australia to try and regain The Ashes. It was regarded by many as a thankless, if not impossible task, for the simple reason that Australia possessed, in the diminutive Don Bradman, the most effective match-winning run machine cricket had seen, or was likely to see. Jardine, however, was not a man to shirk a challenge; rumour had it that Bradman was uncertain, perhaps even flinched, against pace directed at his leg side and Jardine decided this was worth pursuing. It was known that Frank Foster had done extremely well in Australia in 1911/12 bowling left-armed leg-theory – doubtless this knowledge provoked Jardine into meeting Foster in Foster's Belgravia flat, where the main discussion was apparently the type of field Foster set in Australia. This is, this writer feels, something of a mystery since the field used in 1911/12 was no secret and plans had been published at the time, and subsequently. I would not have the impertinence to attempt to match

David Frith's masterly story of the 1932/33 series, in his book *Bodyline Autopsy*, but I feel justified in looking at the matter from Foster's point of view. Certainly he was brought into the bodyline furore. Perhaps I might quote from unpublished notes in my possession, undated but seemingly written by Foster during or after the bodyline series.

A few weeks ago I saw in Australian newspapers that my name had been used in connexion with body-line bowling twenty years ago. There was no such thing as body-line bowling twenty years ago. Some people have said I originated leg-theory bowling. That may be so, but there is a vast difference between leg-theory and body-line. The word body-line was never used by Australian critics when I was bowling but in the last few months they have used it a very great deal and personally I think they have been justified. I will give you my reasons for making that statement.

It is my considered opinion that no right-handed fast bowler should ever attempt to bowl leg-theory. It is dangerous to the batsman, even on the perfect wickets of Australia, and on the best wickets in England. A right-hand fast bowler who sets his field on the leg side immediately becomes a body-line bowler, because the batsman has no time to get away from a short pitched ball. Another point, no left-handed fast bowler should ever bowl over the wicket.[65] If he does, to a leg-side field, he also becomes a body-line bowler. Why? Because a left-arm bowler, bowling over the wicket, cannot possibly see all three stumps.[66] There is only one legitimate way for a fast bowler to bowl leg-theory and get away with it without causing friction and trouble. That bowler must be left handed and must bowl round the wicket. His objective must be leg stump, not the leg of the batsman. A left arm bowler bowling round the wicket is in a position to see all three stumps, and even if he packs the leg side with all his fielders he can never be accused of bowling anything else other than leg-theory if he bowls a good length ball. No fast bowler should ever try to intimidate a batsman by bowling bumpers. A bowler who deliberately bowls short pitched balls cannot by any stretch of the imagination kid himself he is playing cricket. He should be called aside by his captain who should impress upon him that he is not playing the game.'

Foster goes on to reproduce the contents of a personal letter he wrote to the 1933 county captains:

I think you will recognise my name at the end of this letter as being that of an old County Captain, and you will no doubt recall that the English and Australian press of 1933 attributed to me the doubtful honour of originating leg-theory (body-line) bowling on the cricket fields of Australia in 1911/12. I took great exception to this because there is a great difference between leg theory and body-line as I stated in a cable

---

65   This writer did but he was not at all fast!
66   Foster is assuming all batsmen to be right-handers, of course.

on 11 March 1933, to all the Australian newspapers. [See later excerpt from article in *Smith's Weekly* for 18 March.] I have also expressed my view on a Colombia gramophone record DB 1140, with Larwood starring on the other side, whereon I said that it was my considered opinion that there is great danger in body-line bowling. The integrity of English cricket must be above reproach; unfortunately the good name was sadly besmirched in Australia in 1932/33. We must win back that honour.

Foster then suggests the onus be put on the captains to warn, or remove, any of his bowlers seeking to exploit body-line bowling.

Foster also appeared in the Australian press, in the 18 March issue of *Smith's Weekly,* a patriotic weekly tabloid published in Sydney.[67] Under banner headlines 'English Bombshell at Douglas Jardine', Foster was quoted as saying that England 'is shamed by the victory'. The article went on:

> Jardine is welcome to The Ashes, at the price England paid for them. Say this from me to the captain of the England XI in Australia: 'Douglas Jardine, I am ashamed of England's win. I will face you on your return with these words on my lips. You allowed Woodfull to beat you in every sense of the word Cricket. Woodfull won the Second Test by clean methods. We won our four matches by other methods. I take my hat off to Woodfull for resisting the temptation to retaliate in body-line bowling. Cricket history has no finer example of sportsmanship. My name has been used in the body-line controversy, in connection with Warner's tour of 1911/12. I indignantly repudiate the suggestion that I ever used body-line bowling. I have struck men by accident. What fast bowler hasn't? But I never deliberately sent the ball at a batsman's head or body. I aimed always for good length balls. Batsmen like Hobbs or Macartney were never struck by me, because they knew how to use their feet.'

> Being a left-handed bowler, I never once in my whole cricket career bowled over the wicket. A left-arm bowler, bowling over the wicket, immediately becomes a body-liner for he cannot possibly see the three stumps. Body-line bowling is quite different from the leg-theory, which I understand and which I bowled. I am sorry that Nottingham, through Larwood and Voce, figures so conspicuously in the cloud surrounding England's victory.

> Allen has proved himself a perfect gentleman and on his ability and sportsmanship he should be England's captain. Allen displayed strength of character in resisting Jardine's 'body-line' influence. I greatly regret Larwood's actions. As the finest fast bowler England has seen in thirty years he is too good to resort to any kind of leg theory. Unless MCC does uphold the protest from the Australian Board of

---

67   One of its founders was Clyde Packer, grandfather of one Kerry.

Control the game will be ruined in the coming season. Even schoolboy fast bowlers, encountering difficult wickets and expert batsmen will bowl bumpers deliberately at the man instead of the wicket. Body-line bowling must be abolished. The only solution is to give the umpire power to no-ball. And it must be done before the 1934 season, as Jardine may still be captain when the Australians visit us.

The *Smith's Weekly* article then concluded with a comment on P.F.Warner's presence in the visiting party and a revelation regarding the body-line plan. About Warner he said: 'In the whole history of cricket, there have never previously been two managers sent to Australia with an England XI. Warner was sent to keep the peace. The cable sent by the Australian Board of Control is evidence that he failed in his object.'

Foster's final statement concerning Jardine contains the honest indignation of a sportsman who has felt himself misused, or so stated *Smith's Weekly*. 'Before Jardine left England, he came frequently to my flat in St James and secured from me my leg-theory field placings. I had no hint these would be used for body-line bowling. I would like all my old friends in Australian cricket to know that I am sorry that my experience and my advice were put to such unworthy uses.'

Smith's Weekly went on to say that Foster's article was 'the death-knell of bodyline bowling in the minds of all decent sportsmen and in the playing of all decent cricket'. (There are those who would say that had Foster been Australian it would have been thought of as part of a massive whinge.) Australian writer J.C.Davis then gives a short biography of Foster, emphasising Foster's qualifications to speak with 'authority and soundness' on the bodyline matter.

Foster was still not finished. As previously mentioned a gramophone record was made, Foster giving his point of view, Larwood then recording his reply. Through the kindness of David Frith I have heard a tape of the recording. There is little that Foster said which I have not already mentioned above and the sound is so bad that it is hard to work out what Foster is saying, though the slight 'Brummie' accent is apparent. Larwood attempts justification of his bodyline tactics, pleading that he has never bowled at a batsman in his life and that leg-theory is no more unsporting than a batsman playing with his pads. Foster was pleased to note in his unpublished writings that, whereas he wrote his own 'speech', Larwood was scripted by Foster's old adversary E.H.D.Sewell. Foster only knew this when the Columbia recording manager asked him to send a copy of what he intended to say to Sewell. Foster had never met Sewell until now and took the opportunity to ask him why he criticised him and Tiger Smith some twenty years before, but no explanation was recorded.

The English press, by and large, was not well disposed towards Foster in 1933. In the Lord's pressbox during the 1933 Test match he met up with H.J.Henley, of the *Daily Mail*. Foster respected Henley, regarding him as a 'beautiful writer' and a staunch supporter of England. Henley had 'decided views' on bodyline, views not coinciding with those of Foster. When he spotted Foster in the pressbox Henley shouted, 'Get out. You are nothing else but a traitor to your own country.' 'Rats,' replied Foster. 'Well, come and read what M.A.Noble has written about leg theory,' said Henley.

'Go to blazes!' replied Foster to Henley, whom Foster describes as '6 feet 4 inches or so.' Foster went on, 'I do not wish to read what other people write. I know all about the difference between leg-theory and body-line without going to school again. And listen, Falstaff, why do you call me a traitor?'

'Because,' Henley replied, 'you have supported Australia against your own country. I was brought up to understand that once an Englishman, always an Englishman, but you have gone dead against the country in which you were born and bred.' 'Do you frankly mean that a traitor is one who supports right over wrong?' said Foster, seeking to make a pun over his name. 'That is beside the question,' replied Henley, 'and you haven't the slightest idea what went on in Australia in 1932/33, because you were not present.'

'Have you ever been to Australia, Mr Henley?' 'No,' he replied. 'Well, I have and what is more my soul lived there during the last series of murderous Test matches. I am not a traitor, because time will prove that Australia are absolutely correct in their stand against body-line.'

'I think Jardine stuck to his guns well,' said Henley. Foster cut in: 'Listen baby have you ever heard of such a thing as cricket goodwill, because if you have not it is about time you did? England visit Australia as cricket ambassadors, to further goodwill and respect between the countries, not to cause trouble and friction.' Foster went on to say that Australia would not come to England in 1934 unless MCC gave way on bodyline. The debate rather degenerated and, with the rest of the press corps looking on, Henley finally pleaded he had work to do.

The debate was now running out of steam anyway; Foster's last meaningful contribution to cricket was fading away, as indeed was Foster. However one must mention a letter Foster received in March 1933, and which he claims moved him to tears, showing that despite his belligerent attitude in some facets of cricket, and his cheap and shabby private life, he still had a heart. Written from 11 Wellington Road Handsworth Wood and dated 28 March 1933, it reads word for word:

Dear Sir,

I trust you will forgive this intrusion from a perfect stranger, but as a great admirer of Warwickshire's former captain I feel I would like to write and say how greatly I enjoyed *Cricketing Memories*. Owing unfortunately to my being at present out of a position I have been unable to purchase a copy, but had been informed that same could be seen at the Public Library, where I spent a pleasant two hours yesterday.

When Warwickshire won the Championship in 1911, I was then only nine years of age, not old enough I am afraid to appreciate the feat, but nevertheless I can recall my father taking me down to New Street Station when the train returned from Northampton, so I can feel privileged to number myself among those whom you had in mind when writing the book.

I was never a startling success at the game myself, but without attempting any bragging spirit, can pride myself on a knowledge of its fine points, and am acknowledged by my friends as a second *Wisden*. (Even the *Birmingham Mail* have on occasion so far forgot themselves as to publish Test match records I have submitted.)

Since 1913 the number of matches I have missed at Edgbaston could be counted on my fingers, and oft have I sighed for your return. Your remarkable skill at the game, apart from your personality would, I am convinced, have taken Warwicks to the head of the championship table more than once since the war.

When I recall the number of matches that have been 'thrown away' at Edgbaston for the lack of that 'little something' that such as yourself possessed, I could have wept. Please do not think I am attempting flattery, I am quoting cold facts, as a matter of fact I have spoken to you but once, that was in 1913, when you very kindly signed my autograph book, which I still treasure.

Yours very truly,
Norman H. Freeman

Certainly a sad letter and one can understand Foster's being moved. I know nothing of Norman Freeman; unemployment in the early 1930s was rife, and one hopes he eventually found a 'position'. The more enterprising emigrated, left their home area, or became self-employed. What became of Norman Freeman?

Why did Foster come out so strongly against bodyline? Maybe he did genuinely believe in the unsporting nature of that form of attack. Alternatively he was at the time working on a second book of memoirs and perhaps he thought it may do him some good to nail his banner so firmly against bodyline. The new book never appeared in print and having seen Foster's original incomplete typescript and his handwritten notes I can state there was never the slightest possibility of its publication. He was clearly now hopelessly and embarrassingly mentally sick.

In 1934, Foster still thought he had something to offer. Before the Test series began, he told R.E.S.Wyatt that, since he knew how to bowl to Australians, he felt he (Foster) should be chosen for England. Now 45 and with his first-class career twenty years behind him, no longer could he possibly be taken seriously. Even so, as late as February 1937 in a letter to Roy Genders, later a first-class cricketer and author, Foster stated that E.F.Hudson Ltd, booksellers and publishers in New Street, Birmingham, had purchased the 'second book' outright and were keeping it 'in reserve'. In fact it was unpublishable. Foster also harps on about 'the mess Jardine and Larwood made of things in Australia four years ago. Thank goodness Allen is playing square in Australia at the moment. He should bring back The Ashes.' He didn't of course.

Some time after 1932 Foster left London and returned to Birmingham. In 1933 he occupied a luxury flat at 111 Hagley Road West, Quinton. He shared this with three females, one of whom was his wife, Norah Gladys Foster, by then the mother of three children, who had allegedly been estranged from her husband three years earlier. The other occupants were Annie Rose Davis, perhaps born in Cheltenham in 1871, and Annie Gertrude James, probably born in London in 1899, both probably domestic staff. By 1934 he was living with Norah Foster at No.1 in a block of 21 flats at Westfield Hall on Hagley Road. It is near the Chad Valley area and it is possible, though unlikely, that the wrecked motor-cycle legend mentioned in Chapter Eight had some substance and that somehow and for some reason he carted the bike to his new Birmingham address. By 1935 Norah had gone, having been replaced by Ada Ashen, probably born at Northend in the parish of Ratley in Warwickshire in 1902, presumably 'a domestic'. Ada was still with Foster in 1940 but died in 1943.

Going back 'home' was not the happy return Foster would have hoped for. He continued living beyond his means, thereby running up debts. Inevitably this road led to disaster and in 1936 he was forced to file for bankruptcy, with a Receiving Order made against him.

The Public Examination, in front of Registrar Glanfield was heard on 2 September 1936 in Birmingham County Court. Foster was represented by Mr T.F.Mason, of solicitors Glaisyer, Porter and Mason. Foster attributed his failure to 'betting on horses and dog racing and extravagance in living.' His age was given as 47 and the statement of affairs showed gross liabilities of £631 8s 4d, with £628 12s 9d expected to rank for dividend. Assets were expected to produce £27 4s 5d leaving a deficit of £601 8s 4d.[68]

The Registrar heard that for twenty years before 1928, with the exception of a short period of war service, Foster was employed by the family clothing firm Foster Brothers,[69] latterly as a superintendent of ten branch shops at £4,000 per year. Owing to differences he left the firm and until January 1930 he received an allowance of £2,000 per year. Since that time, on his becoming separated from his wife, his allowance had been reduced to £1,100, with the balance going to his estranged wife and children. He had been betting on horse and dog racing for twenty years and he estimated a loss of £500 on betting during the past two years. A bookmaker was the petitioning creditor. The unsecured liabilities included

---

68   £601 is worth around £22,500 in 2011 values.
69   This was not quite accurate since, until the death of his father in 1914, Foster had worked for Wilkinson and Riddell in central Birmingham, a firm with no connection with Foster Brothers (Clothing) Limited.

£353 14s 6d for betting from early 1934 until June 1936. The balance of £274 18s 3d was mainly for household expenses.

In reply to Mr Kynoch Clark, the Official Receiver, Foster said that in 1921 he had £5,000 worth of shares in the Foster Brothers clothing company. He got into difficulties and his mother found a sum of money and he signed over the shares to her. He could not recall how much of his liabilities his mother satisfied in consideration for receiving the shares. He admitted he had not included debts of about £500 in his statement of affairs. It was an oversight since he had not heard of the accounts for more than two years.

Foster stated he was captaining Warwickshire in 1911 and went with the MCC side to Australia. The Official Receiver then asked: 'Is it not true to say that your circumstances then resulted in your acquiring extravagant habits?' Foster replied: 'No, I shouldn't like to say so. My people have always had money and I have always had good money from the business.'

Official Receiver: 'For two years you have been living beyond your means?' Foster replied: 'I would not say that. I lost money through betting.' The Official Receiver, perhaps slightly exasperated, then asked: 'How long have you been living beyond your means?' Foster: 'It is difficult to say because of the racing.' He added that except for the racing he had been living within his means. Mr Mason, Foster's solicitor, asked him when he thought he had started living beyond his means. He replied that in 1934 he realised he was living outside his income and he got into difficulties. As a result he tried to make his income up through betting.

Mr Mason then asked: 'Is it not true that at one time you were going to make betting your business?' Foster: 'I did take it up as a business.' Mason: 'And you now see the folly of it?' Foster: 'Yes,' Mason: 'And you have given it up and will continue to do so?' Foster: 'Yes, I have given it up.'

The Registrar concluded the hearing, pending Foster signing the transcript of the hearing as a true and accurate record.[70]

---

70   Cricket statistician Glyn Powell, a former employee of the Official Receiver's office, says that it is almost certain Foster never applied for his bankruptcy discharge so died a bankrupt. Had he lived until Section 7 of the Insolvency Act 1976 came into force, granting automatic discharge to all bankruptcies of five years or more, he would have been released.

Chapter Ten

The cloudy days of autumn and of winter

It is believed that Foster remained in Birmingham throughout the war, and was definitely still at the Hagley Road flat in 1944. However in 1946 he certainly rung the changes. A letter dated 10 May, to one Norman Malyon of Walthamstow, gives Foster's address as 33 Bury Street, St. James, round the corner from his address in 1931: 'I have moved to a bigger place'. He tells Malyon he has lost the photos he had sent him to sign ('cuss it!') and then carries on with some incomprehensible comments about dogs. Thirteen days later he wrote again to Malyon. The letter commences: 'Yes I played with and against Gilbert Jessop, he can't help it, neither can C.B.Fry another thing like that. Alright send him running to me, I'll make him sign! I cannot find that photo cutting yet and maybe one of the maids pinched it off my table. I moved because I was losing things from my mom. How glad I am. I am home at last here, and they are charming people.' He then lists his first four for the forthcoming Epsom Derby, reckoning he will get them at 500-1. He finishes by informing the recipient that he is going to Australia for the 1946/47 Ashes tour to report the Tests. 'England will win the Rubber 5-0.' Steve Musk, author of the *Lives in Cricket* book on Michael Falcon remarks: 'thieving maids, losing things – some evidence of paranoia perhaps?' Also his forecast of the Ashes result, and the statement he will be in Australia reporting shows no grasp of reality.

On 8 June, Foster writes to 'Norman's Dad' from another new address, 41 Hertford Street, a large house in Mayfair: 'I am terribly sorry, got stuck in Baker Street until 5 pm; could not move and I cussed like 'ell. [*sic*] A bobby said, "Are you talking to me?" That did it! I laughed like nobody's business. Please note change of address. Wot! Again!' 'A somewhat eccentric letter,' reckons Steve Musk, as well he might.

Another strange thing is that, on 10 June, Foster wrote to Malyon from yet another address, 46 Clarges Street, just off Piccadilly. It was one of a furnished service suite. Three addresses in a few days? Just what was happening? And what a strange letter:

Look Norman, this is the day. Went to the fight last night with a priest. Bruce is a world beater, yes sir.[71] Have just put an offer through for a

---

71   Bruce Woodcock, who had just outpointed Freddie Mills at Harringay for the British heavyweight title. Despite Foster's optimism Woodcock always fell well short on the world stage. When Woodcock touched gloves with challenger Jack Gardner for the British 'and Empire' heavyweight titles at Earl's Court in 1950, one boxing insider remarked: 'Well, a straight title fight; we'll see what he's made of now.' Gardner hammered him to defeat and retirement.

Turf Accountants, going concern off the Edgware Road. If you like figures, and good ones, now is your chance. 1 tape, a phone, and 2 blondes. I expect a partner, and you. Eh? Is it on? We open Friday, 7th. You had better phone me or come here before 11 o'clock any morning.

Have sent the photos to Gilbert J.[72] They are jolly fine. Yes, he was the best ever. My very finest bowling performance was against him at Edgbaston. I bowled two maiden overs at him and then Frank Field knocked his castle over.

Can you type, or do you know someone who does? If I go to Australia I think the office will be ok, with Jackie Dane, Music Hall comedian and Reg Seabright, the great amateur boxer. I shall want a good typist.

Yours ever
Frank

Among other things, it seems he was thinking of setting up a bookmaking business, despite being an undischarged bankrupt, even though he was about to travel to Australia to report on the Test series. There is no detail about Norman's response to this.

The letters quoted above show evidence of a sad and confused individual, but the saddest happening of 1946 will be seen in a terse entry in the committee minutes of Warwickshire County Cricket Club, dated 22 October 1946: 'It was reluctantly decided that in view of his disgraceful conduct on several occasions during the past season, notably towards amateur players and members of the catering staff, that F.R.Foster be refused admission to the ground in future.'

What a thing to happen to a former captain and playing hero: unfortunately I have found it very hard to obtain further information.

Although I never asked specifically about this matter, Leslie Deakins, the splendid and long-serving County Club secretary seemed reluctant to speak about Foster in the years long before I decided to write this biography, though he did once say that 'he was a sad case'. Perhaps Leslie was simply too nice a chap with regard to such things. What can be said is that Frank Foster's great-nephew Nigel Foster is aware of at least one incident during the season, details of which were passed to him by amateur allrounder Jack Marshall. Apparently Foster, in drink taken, thought he was captaining the side and started to hand out orders even, possibly, attempting to take the field. Jeanne Dollery, widow of Tom Dollery, did not recall this but was aware of some sort of incident between Foster and professional allrounder Bill Fantham during the 1946 season. All involved with the running of Warwicks cricket in 1946 are now dead and since nothing was published at the time it seems most unlikely the proper story will see light of day. It is doubtful Foster ever again visited Edgbaston and

---

72   Almost certainly the old Gloucestershire and England player, G.L.Jessop.

one cannot countenance a worse end to his connections with the County Club.[73]

Foster did not linger long in London – possibly he was running short of landlords to take him on. Perhaps credit-worthiness, or lack of it, militated against him.

In any event 1950 finds him living at 8 Nelson Road, Leigh-on-Sea, an undistinguished end-of-terrace house near Chalkwell Park cricket ground, where Essex played an annual festival. Warwicks did not appear there until 1954 however, when Foster was long gone. Whatever Foster's situation, he was up to his old tricks, as a letter to Rego Clothing Company of Oxford Street, Marble Arch shows. It was dated 26 June 1950, an important date, as will be seen, and which makes the contents almost beyond belief:

> Sirs,
>
> Yes, alright I'll try a few of your grey sports shirts. It certainly looks a very good idea, and I know what I'm talking about as I am the retired boss of Foster Brothers Clothing Co. Ltd, Birmingham. 150 branches. I will take half a dozen, collar size 17 and a half, Light grey, medium grey, 2 gold, light Blue, Saxe Blue. You may also send me three silk mufflers to match up. And your latest catalogue please.
>
> Yours Truly,
> Frank R.Foster, Warwickshire and England Cricketer

The grammar is erratic and one is surprised Rego allowed his order apparently without checking. Days later Rego replied they had nothing large enough in the line but one of their directors, Mr Spragg, was procuring enough of the material to make the shirts up. The mufflers were in stock and would be reserved until the shirts were finished. The letter finishes 'May I, an ardent cricket fan express the hope that you are in the best of health, and remain, yours faithfully.'

On 17 July the firm informed Foster that the specially made shirts would be delivered in a day or two and asked if he would prefer them and the mufflers to be sent C.O.D. The details were six shirts at £1 7s 6d, three mufflers at 17s 11d, and their total value £10 18s 9d. Three days later: 'Goods herewith as arranged over phone, together with statement. Trusting you are soon recovered from your indisposition.' Finally on 1 August: 'I am pleased to hear that the goods supplied met with your approval, and am very interested to learn you have such a promising protégé. An outstanding man is sorely needed at the present time.' Then, ominously, 'We are enclosing a statement for the goods supplied and your cheque will oblige.' It is surely a rhetorical question to ask whether it was paid.

---

73   However it helps not at all to read in Wikipedia that he 'continued to watch the game until his death'. It will shortly emerge that this was not just untrue, but impossible. Just where does such 'information' emanate?

Do Not Pass 'Go'.
In 1946, Foster lived in Clarges Steet, Mayfair (left) but by 1950 had moved to Nelson Road, Leigh-on-Sea (right).
Charles James Fox, Whig Foreign Secretary, once lived in the Mayfair house.
Both pictures taken in 2010.

The most remarkable facet of this series of correspondence is that on 27 June, a day after Foster's first letter to Rego above he wrote the following somewhat pathetic epistle to a branch of Midland Bank in Birmingham:

Dear Mr Rossier,

Elizabeth Foster, dec.[74]

I have to thank you very much indeed for your extreme kindness in sending the money to the Midland Bank at Leigh-on-Sea. There was no letter awaiting me at the bank, and I received no letter this morning. Am I to take it you are sending me the full £150 on Friday to the same bank, because if you do I shall never forget the goodness that you have all shown me since the death of my dearly beloved mother. Practically all the money I received yesterday has gone paying the most urgent bills, but there is still one very important account to settle and that is a loan on my car.

I had a visit yesterday from two CID men about this very account and they gave me rather a rough overhauling, with the threat of reporting the matter to the Chief Constable. I did my best and we parted on a fairly friendly basis, but as they left one man said 'We will do our best for you, but it is a very serious matter and I think you will see us again.' Mr Rossier, I don't want any more trouble in my life. I have had enough of it. For the last time, and I mean it, I beg of you to help me by sending

---

74   Foster's mother.

the £150 cheque on Friday. If my account is overdrawn, I will pay you in some way.

Yours very truly
Frank R.Foster

This is the last letter to be mentioned in this book. Further comment would be superfluous.

On 18 August, at Southend Magistrates' Court, Foster appeared on thirteen charges of larceny and intent to defraud. It was alleged he stole a car and defrauded taxi drivers by giving worthless cheques for fares, mostly for trips from London to Leigh-on-Sea. Through his solicitor, Mr J.C.Lamb, Foster pleaded 'Not Guilty' and was remanded for trial at the next Southend Quarter Sessions. Detective Inspector Todd opposed bail. He stated Foster should have appeared a few days earlier. Foster's explanation for his non-appearance was that he had had to go to London to tell the MCC about a twenty-year-old left-arm fast bowler called Ron Bumstead. Foster said there would be 'a Hell of a row' if Bumstead were not chosen for the 1950/51 MCC Ashes tour to Australia. With Bumstead in the side Foster reckoned England would win the series 5-0, a result he had forecast for the 1946/47 series, with similar inaccuracy. England lost 4-1 in 1950/51 and whether Bumstead would have affected the result is doubtful. One has to comment that despite efforts from several sources it has been impossible to trace any cricketer of that name. Foster claimed to have been in touch with MCC by post with regard to Bumstead but Lord's has no file on the matter. Foster's bail application was refused.[75]

Later that day the same magistrates heard another case, again involving Foster, that he assaulted John Beale, a County Court bailiff, in the execution of his duty. Beale was trying to execute a warrant on Foster's goods and chattels at his home, 8 Nelson Road, Leigh-on-Sea. Beale alleged Foster threw a cigarette in his face, raised a cane as if to hit him, and finally punched Beale in the face. Foster said he had no intention of hitting the bailiff but when he refused to leave the house he had struck him. The court fined Foster £5, with three guineas costs. Prosecuting counsel requested that if Foster could not immediately pay he should be sent to prison, at which Mr Lamb, Foster's solicitor, jumped forward and paid it for him. For this act of charity Foster said, 'Thank you, sir'.

The *Southend Standard* reported that during the court hearings Foster was shown a picture of a young man in cricket kit and defending solicitor asked him to identify the man shown. He replied: 'That's me. I played for England in 1912 and for Warwickshire in '11, '12, '13 and '14.' Asked about the tie he was wearing, he replied that it was an England tie and only men who had played cricket for England were allowed to wear it. He said he had captained England against Tasmania in 1932 [*sic*].

---

75   There is no trace of a cricketer named Bumstead playing successfully, or at all, in Essex or Southend newspapers at around this time.

Foster's next court appearance was on 26 September at Southend Quarter Sessions. He changed his plea to 'Guilty' through counsel. Mr George Pollock, for Foster, said that in his day Foster had been a great cricketer, but his head had been turned by admiration. His mother, on her death, had left an estate worth £300,000, of which Foster's share had been approximately £7,000 per annum. Foster was reported to have been receiving £150 a month, which sounds an unlikely sum. 'Money flowed from him like water in a brook.' He acquired a number of so-called friends, of whom a better description would have been 'spongers'. Mr Pollock said Foster clearly needed protection because he had become a nuisance to people. The sum involved here had been £115 9s 6d, of which practically the whole amount had been paid back by the trustees of his mother's estate.

After hearing medical evidence, the Recorder announced he was placing Foster on twelve months probation on condition that he became a voluntary hospital patient. It was stated that Foster, 'grey bearded but upright' bowed to the Recorder as he consented to the discharge conditions. So Foster was escorted to St Andrew's Psychiatric Hospital in Northampton and he is not known to have left until his death nearly eight years later. His record card, but no file, survives to this day. This states merely that he was 'a psychopath'; no medical training was needed for that diagnosis.

Chapter Eleven
And winter fought her battle strife and won

St Andrew's Hospital, Billing Road, Northampton is a psychiatric hospital, of some 600 beds and cares for all forms of mental illness. Founded in 1838 as the 'Northamptonshire County General Lunatic Asylum', it is these days run by a non-profit-making charity. Over the years there have been distinguished patients, additional to Frank Foster. Sir Malcolm Arnold, amongst the finest of English twentieth-century composers had treatment there in 1979 for depression and alcoholism. Josef Hassad, rated by good judges the greatest violin genius for 200 years when a teenager, died there in 1950, aged 26. The architect George Gilbert Scott and poet James Kenneth Stephen, a relation of Virginia Woolf, were other residents but the most relevant to the Foster story, was the 'Peasant Poet', John Clare, who spent his last 23 years there and whose poem *Remembrances*, written while he was a mental patient supplied the inspiration for the title of this book.

The question may be asked from what specific mental illness Frank Foster suffered. A psychiatrist's report read to the Recorder at the final court hearing suggested senile dementia. This may be the case but perhaps there could be doubt, especially when Foster's history is examined. I was told by former Warwicks and England wicket-keeper, Tiger Smith, in his nineties, that Foster's downhill slide began on a night in Melbourne during 1911/12. Smith did not, or would not elaborate on the matter but given that Foster was almost certainly sexually promiscuous, one feels that Smith referred to a dalliance with a woman – and an unhealthy one. One also remembers that in his writings, published and unpublished, Foster expressed great sympathy for Warwickshire batsman Sep Kinneir, who most certainly suffered from syphilis early in his cricket career. This, and the treatment, left him with deep-seated and permanent physical and mental damage. Then there was the inarguable fact that, from the early 1920s, Foster's behaviour became progressively more eccentric and erratic. That surely could not be passed off as *senile* dementia. Also sexual disease was 'in the family'. His ne'er-do-well brother, Arthur, received treatment for gonorrhoea and syphilis during his First World War army service.

Finally, although the death certificate gives 'cardiovascular degeneration' and 'chronic anaemia' as causes of death, I cannot believe there was not more to the matter. Though not really qualified to offer an opinion, I do have views. I feel it is possible that in later years, Foster suffered from general paralysis of the insane (known as GPI) and although understandably he does not wish to be named, an acquaintance, a

*St Andrew's Hospital, Northampton.
Foster was an in-patient here from 1950 until his death in 1958.*

professional psychiatrist admits of the likelihood. GPI is a mental disorder occurring in tertiary syphilis and was once known as dementia paralytica. In its last stages it can cause damage to the heart and blood vessels (thus cardiovascular degeneration) and brain, and progressive paralysis. Early symptoms include depression, personality change and lack of inhibitions. The disease may take many years to develop. I am not suggesting that GPI was the major reason for Frank Foster's physical and mental collapse, and his death, but it ticks some boxes.

In any event Frank Foster died at St Andrew's on 3 May 1958.

Foster's remains were interred in the family plot at Brandwood End Cemetery, King's Heath, Birmingham on 9 May 1958, after a short service in the cemetery chapel conducted by Canon Norman Power.[76] A small family representation was there, including his children, but no-one from the cricket world in general. Perhaps it had been convenient to 'forget'. Certainly Warwickshire County Cricket Club seems to have held this view. The Yearbook had a deserved reputation for honouring its departed players, and even better-known or long-serving members. Yet the passing of Frank Foster – arguably its greatest-ever cricketer, probably its finest and most successful captain, the club's first cricket hero, the man who in a playing sense had put the county on the map – was, apart from a few lines, ignored. If it wasn't an editorial oversight, then surely it was inexcusable small-mindedness.[77]

---

76   Canon Power was himself a good cricketer. Once, in partnership with his brother Alan he added nearly 200 for the Birmingham Clergy against 'The Doctors' at Edgbaston.

77   A few years later however a new road near the Edgbaston ground was named 'Foster Way'. On the same estate we find 'Dollery Drive', 'Wyatt Close', 'Hollies Croft' and 'Wickets Tower'. Retaining the cricket theme, nearby is 'Calthorpe Road' while a good walk away is 'Shilton Grove.'

The death did not pass completely unnoticed. Some mundane obituaries appeared in the press but the daughter of the late Warwicks secretary, R.V.Ryder, said what should have been said elsewhere – the ideal epitaph. When asked for her memories, Margaret Abbot wrote:

> Was there ever a hero worshipped more in his day by the very young? His name became a legend, without the bolstering up by television or radio. After all these years I recall childhood memories, still fresh and vivid at the spell he cast around him. We were enthralled when F.R.Foster went out to bat. Anything could happen. Where might he not send them? Yes, that went for six, right over Edgbaston Road and into Queen's Drive. And then they carried him shoulder-high off the field, the autograph hunters around him.

Frank Foster was buried in the family plot in Brandwood End Cemetery, a couple of miles from his childhood home at Mel Valley.

Acknowledgements

I am grateful to the ACS, for publishing this biography and especially to its editor David Jeater for giving me my 'head' when at times he may have had his doubts. David also took photographs in London and Essex and examined Essex newspapers for reports of Frank Foster's various 'problems'. This is, I hope you will agree, like no other cricketing biography – not only because of the eccentric style of the author. It is several years since I realised there was much more to Frank Foster than the 'official' version – a fine allrounder whose career was cut short by a road accident – and after being advised by someone in cricket for whom I had the highest respect to 'let him rest in peace', I offered it to the ACS.

I am extremely grateful to my mate Steve Sheen for the amount of help he has given me – especially when glaucoma made it difficult to undertake vital further research via microfilm. Thanks also to Peter Wynne-Thomas for helping out after personal reasons forced me to dispose of most of my cricket library, though 'research' visits to Trent Bridge did tend to degenerate into 80% nattering time. Then there is Stephen Chalke who, although he felt he could not publish my work in the form I wanted, did encourage me and suggest the title; David Frith, who sent me a tape of Foster's 'bodyline' speech in 1933 and also encouraged in other ways; and Charlie Wat, who really put himself out researching Australian sources.

Those were the major helpers: there are others who helped, some without knowing, and whom I now list, in no particular order: John Loynton, historian of Solihull School; Bob Blackham of the Tolkien Society; Brian Halford, George Dobell, Nigel Foster, Tony Robinson, Glyn Powell, Steve Musk, Neil Duggan, Ken Birrell, Josephine Cooper, Steve Williams, Bobbie Judd, Arthur Wentworth, my late cousin Michael Carroll, David Foot, Dr Paul Lester; M.J.K.Smith, a former captain of Warwickshire, and now president of the ACS, who contributed the foreword; and Pete Griffiths, with whose organisation CricketArchive I was able to check statistics. In addition to these I have made good use of the resources of the Birmingham Central and Solihull public libraries and the British Library newspaper collection at Colindale.

For their part in the production of the book, my thanks go to Pete Griffiths, who has overseen the production process and attended to the complexities of typesetting; City Press who have designed the cover; Roger Mann and Steve Sheen, for their help with illustrations; and to Gerald Hudd and David Pracy who have contributed their proofreading skills.

Finally – Frank Foster. If I am going to be surprised, and there is a hereafter, and Frank is able to look down on me, I hope he will not be too displeased, and will agree that his story had to be told. In any event, though not exactly liking him, I did sympathise.

Knowle, Warwickshire
January, 2011

Select Bibliography

1 Regular publications

Cricket magazine, 1907 to 1913
The Cricketer magazine, 1921 to 1950
The Cricket Statistician magazine, 1971 to 1995
Warwickshire County Cricket Club, *Annual Reports*, 1907 to 1958
Wisden Cricketers' Almanack, 1907 to 1976
World of Cricket magazine, 1914

2 Books

Barker, Ralph and Irving Rosenwater, *England v Australia, 1877–1968*, Batsford, 1969
Blackham, Robert, *The Roots of Tolkien's Middle Earth*, The History Press, 2006
Brooke, Robert, *Warwickshire County Cricket Club: 100 Greats*, Tempus, 2001
Brooke, Robert and David Goodyear, *A Who's Who of Warwickshire County Cricket*, Robert Hale, 1989
Brooke, Robert, *Warwickshire CCC First-Class Records, 1894–1993*, Limlow Books, 1994
Carpenter, Humphrey, *J.R.R.Tolkien: A Biography*, Harper Collins, 1978
Douglas, Christopher, *Douglas Jardine: Spartan Cricketer*, Methuen, 2003
Duckworth, Leslie, *The Story of Warwickshire Cricket*, Stanley Paul, 1985
Foot, David, *Cricket's Unholy Trinity*, Stanley Paul, 1985
Foster, Frank R., *Cricketing Memories*, London Publishing Co Ltd, 1930
Foster, Frank R., *My Cricketing Life*, unpublished
Frith, David, *Bodyline Autopsy*, Aurum Press, 2003
Frith, David, *Silence of the Heart: Cricket Suicides*, Mainstream Publishing, 2001
Griffiths, Barry, *A Warwickshire Cricket Chronicle*, Lewes Book Guild, 1985
Hobbs, J.B., *Recovering The Ashes*, Pitman, 1912
Scott, John, *Caught in Court*, André Deutsch, 1988
Webster, Ray, *First-Class Cricket in Australia: Vol I, 1850/51–1941/42*, the author, 1991

3 Archive Material

Warwickshire County Cricket Club, Committee Minutes

4 Websites

www.cricketarchive.com

Appendix One
Career Statistics

Test cricket: Batting and Fielding

		M	I	NO	R	HS	Ave	100	50	Ct
1911/12	Australia	5	7	0	226	71	32.28	-	3	2
1912	South Africa	3	4	0	49	30	12.25	-	-	7
1912	Australia	3	4	1	55	20	18.33	-	-	2
Totals		**11**	**15**	**1**	**330**	**71**	**23.57**	**-**	**3**	**11**

Test cricket: Bowling

		O	M	R	W	BB	Ave	5i
1911/12	Australia	276.4	58	692	32	21.62	6/91	3
1912	SA	92.1	32	184	11	16.72	5/16	1
1912	Australia	39	18	50	2	25.00	2/42	-
Total		**407.5**	**108**	**926**	**45**	**20.57**	**6/91**	**4**

First-class cricket: Batting and Fielding

	M	I	NO	R	HS	Ave	100	50	Ct
1908	5	6	1	24	9*	4.80	-	-	1
1909	18	28	4	541	97	22.54	-	3	15
1910	24	40	1	611	77	15.66	-	4	24
1911	23	40	2	1614	200	42.47	3	10	12
1911/12	13	19	1	641	158	35.61	2	3	7
1912	29	47	3	828	70	18.81	-	3	25
1913	22	38	2	829	111	23.02	1	5	14
1914	25	45	3	1460	305*	34.76	1	7	23
Totals	**159**	**263**	**17**	**6548**	**305***	**26.61**	**7**	**35**	**121**

Notes: Foster was dismissed 129 times caught (52%), 90 times bowled (37%), 16 times stumped (7%), eight times lbw (3%) and three times run out (1%). He was dismissed most often by G.E.Dennett, J.A.Newman and S.G.Smith (eight times), and by Wilfred Rhodes and W.C.Smith (seven times).

First-class cricket: Bowling

	O	M	R	W	BB	Ave	5i	10m
1908	170.5	44	397	23	17.26	5-36	1	-
1909	488.2	110	1356	49	27.67	6-46	1	-
1910	873	202	2374	112	21.19	6-51	8	1
1911	952.5	184	2864	141	20.31	9-118	10	3
1911/12	486.1	110	1252	62	20.19	7-36	5	-

1912	858.3	273	2019	116	17.40	7-21	12	3
1913	839.3	198	2345	92	25.48	6-62	7	-
1914	879.4	215	2272	122	18.62	6-18	9	1
Total	**5548.5**	**1336**	**14879**	**717**	**20.75**	**9-118**	**53**	**8**

Notes: Overs were of six balls throughout Foster's first-class career. He took his wickets at the rate of one per 46.43 balls and conceded runs at the rate of 2.68 per over. Of his 717 wickets, 407 (57%, an exceptional proportion) were bowled; 250 (35%) were caught; 44 (6%) were lbw, 16 (2%) were stumped and one hit wicket. Among top pace bowlers, I have found only C.J.Kortright (65%), A.W.Mold (60%), Schofield Haigh (59%) and Tom Richardson (57%) to beat or equal Foster, in the proportion of his 'bowled' dismissals. He took the wickets of nine batsmen eight or more times; these were G.H.Hirst, C.P.Mead and F.E.Wooley (10); Wilfred Rhodes (nine); and Warren Bardsley, F.L.Bowley, S.W.A.Cadman, J.W.H.Makepeace and Arthur Morton (eight).

First-class cricket: Centuries (7)

Score	For	Opponent	Venue	Season
105	Warwickshire[1]	Yorkshire	Edgbaston	1911
200	Warwickshire[1]	Surrey	Edgbaston	1911
101	Warwickshire[2]	Yorkshire	Harrogate	1911
158	MCC[1]	South Australia	Adelaide	1911/12
101	MCC[1]	Victoria	Melbourne	1911/12
111	Warwickshire[2]	Hampshire	Southampton	1913
305*	Warwickshire[1]	Worcestershire	Dudley	1914

Note: His triple century took 257 minutes and included 44 fours and 1 five.

First-Class cricket: Five wickets or more in an innings (53)

Bowling	For	Opponent	Venue	Season
17-6-36-5	Warwickshire	Lancashire[1]	Blackpool	1908
20-6-46-6	Warwickshire	Gloucestershire[1]	Edgbaston	1909
24-3-95-5	Warwickshire	Worcestershire[1]	Worcester	1910
26-5-58-6	Warwickshire	Sussex[1]	Leamington Spa	1910
22-2-87-5	Warwickshire	Leicestershire[2]	Coventry (Bulls Head)	1910
29.2-7-64-5	Warwickshire	Gloucestershire[2]	Gloucester (Spa)	1910
28.1-10-62-5	Warwickshire	Derbyshire[1]	Blackwell	1910
31-12-65-6	Warwickshire	Derbyshire[1]	Edgbaston	1910
22.2-3-51-6	Warwickshire	Derbyshire[2]	Edgbaston	1910
24-4-83-5	Gentlemen	Players[1]	Scarborough	1910
15.3-3-40-6	Warwickshire	Sussex[1]	Coventry (Bulls Head)	1910
29.3-4-118-9	Warwickshire	Yorkshire[1]	Edgbaston	1911
16-5-31-5	Warwickshire	Indians[1]	Edgbaston	1911
31.3-3-76-7	England	The Rest[1]	Lord's	1911
11.4-4-25-5	Warwickshire	Northamptonshire[2]	Edgbaston	1911
15-3-52-5	Warwickshire	Sussex[2]	Chichester	1911
22.2-5-76-5	Warwickshire	Gloucestershire[1]	Edgbaston	1911
22-8-37-6	Warwickshire	Derbyshire[2]	Edgbaston	1911
13.2-6-18-5	Warwickshire	Northamptonshire[1]	Northampton	1911
25-6-63-6	Warwickshire	Northamptonshire[2]	Northampton	1911
19-9-31-6	MCC	Queensland[2]	Brisbane (Gabba)	1911/12
31.3-5-92-5	England	Australia[2]	Sydney	1911/12
38-9-91-6	England	Australia[2]	Melbourne	1911/12
26-9-36-5	England	Australia[1]	Adelaide	1911/12

19.3-6-36-7	MCC	New South Wales[1]	Sydney	1911/12
24-7-55-5	Warwickshire	Sussex[1]	Edgbaston	1912
26.2-4-72-6	Warwickshire	Worcestershire[1]	Dudley	1912
22-6-59-5	Warwickshire	Worcestershire[2]	Dudley	1912
34-10-94-7	Warwickshire	Australians[1]	Edgbaston	1912
13.1-7-16-5	England	South Africa[1]	Lord's	1912
16.5-4-71-5	Warwickshire	Leicestershire[1]	Nuneaton (CC)	1912
19.2-11-21-7	Warwickshire	Leicestershire[2]	Nuneaton (CC)	1912
14-4-22-5	Warwickshire	Northamptonshire[1]	Edgbaston	1912
34-18-58-5	Warwickshire	Middlesex[1]	Edgbaston	1912
21.4-12-29-6	Warwickshire	Middlesex[2]	Edgbaston	1912
19.5-8-42-7	Warwickshire	Yorkshire[1]	Hull	1912
16.5-3-53-6	Warwickshire	Surrey[1]	Edgbaston	1912
20-5-54-5	Warwickshire	Derbyshire[1]	Derby	1913
25.3-4-95-5	Warwickshire	Hampshire[1]	Southampton	1913
29-8-62-6	Warwickshire	Kent[1]	Tonbridge	1913
25.1-6-69-5	Warwickshire	Yorkshire[1]	Sheffield (Bramall Lane) 1913	
27.2-4-76-6	Warwickshire	Worcestershire[1]	Edgbaston	1913
22.5-2-75-6	Warwickshire	Gloucestershire[2]	Cheltenham College 1913	
31-9-73-5	Warwickshire	Northamptonshire[1]	Northampton	1913
28.2-6-69-5	Warwickshire	Leicestershire[1]	Edgbaston	1914
18-6-18-6	Warwickshire	Derbyshire[1]	Edgbaston	1914
14-5-19-5	Warwickshire	Lancashire[2]	Edgbaston	1914
24.5-3-72-5	Warwickshire	Sussex[1]	Nuneaton (CC)	1914
27-10-63-6	Warwickshire	Hampshire[1]	Edgbaston	1914
24-4-78-5	Warwickshire	Hampshire[2]	Edgbaston	1914
23-8-47-5	Warwickshire	Derbyshire[1]	Derby	1914
26-11-53-5	Warwickshire	Kent[2]	Gravesend	1914
27.4-7-48-5	Warwickshire	Surrey[2]	Edgbaston	1914

Note: The index figures [1] and [2] in this and the preceding table indicate the innings in which the feat was achieved.

Warwickshire Captain

Warwickshire won 35 (39.77%) of the 88 matches in which Foster led them. Among regular skippers only D.A.Reeve (43% of 60 matches) exceeds him. H.E.Dollery's record was 36.27% of victories in 215 matches. Foster's record of 70% of results in his 88 matches is best of all. Among irregular captains, with a qualification of 40 games, bottom of the list is D.L.Amiss, who won only five of his 44 matches.

Sources: www.cricketarchive.com and *Wisden's Cricketers' Almanack*.

Appendix Two
The Foster Family

Information not given in the body of the book:

John Foster (grandfather), 1829-1921; a Lincolnshire farmer who later lived at Nuneaton, Warwickshire.

Ann Foster (grandmother), 1829-1921; wife of the above.

Elizabeth Foster (née Rowbotham) (mother), 1860-1943; chairman of Foster Brothers Ltd, 1918-1943

Harry Foster (oldest brother), 1880-1960; ed King Edward's School, Birmingham; managing director of Foster Brothers Ltd, 1919-1950; vice-president of Warwickshire C.C.C.; presented an engraved cigarette box in memory of F.R.Foster to the club in 1960; his daughter Pamela married T.L.Robinson, who played four matches for Warwickshire in 1946.

Edgar Foster (brother), 1899-1977; ed The Leys School, Cambridge; director of Foster Brothers Ltd; played rugby union for Moseley; well known for diving exploits, including in 1953 a dive of 80ft into New York Harbour from sun deck of Queen Elizabeth, another time did same from top deck of Mauretania but record was 97ft from the liner Orama and at age 73 made 33ft dive at Fairfax Street Baths, Coventry, while saluting, to aid a fund for a kidney machine at Queen Elizabeth Hospital, Birmingham in memory of David Parsons of Acocks Green who died in 1970.

David William Foster (son), 1916-2008; ed Repton School, playing in cricket XI 1932-1934, as right hand bat and off-break bowler; lieutenant in King's Light Infantry in Second World War; later Welfare Officer at Brecon; had two daughters.

John Pritchard Foster (son), 1918-2006; played tennis for Warwickshire. captain in Royal Artillery in Second World War; managing director of Foster Brothers Ltd, 1961-73; had two daughters.

Elizabeth Foster (later Armstrong and then Hall) (daughter), 1925-2003; had three sons and one daughter.

Index

A page number in bold indicates an illustration.